The Political
Tales and Truth
of Mark Twain

Edited and with an Introduction by

DAVID HODGE
and
STACEY FREEMAN

THE CLASSIC WISDOM COLLECTION
NEW WORLD LIBRARY
SAN RAFAEL, CALIFORNIA

© 1992 by David Hodge and Stacey Freeman

The Classic Wisdom Collection
Published by New World Library
58 Paul Drive, San Rafael, CA 94903

Cover design: Greg Wittrock
Text design: Nancy Benedict
Typography: Wilsted & Taylor

Excerpts from EUROPE AND ELSEWHERE by Mark Twain. Copyright 1923 by the Mark Twain Company. Copyright renewed 1951 by the Mark Twain Company. Reprinted by permission of HarperCollins Publishers.

Library of Congress Cataloging-in-Publication Data

Twain, Mark, 1835–1910.
    The political tales and truth of Mark Twain / edited
and with an introduction by David Hodge and Stacey
Freeman.
        p.   cm.—(The classic wisdom collection)
    Includes bibliographical references.
    ISBN 1-880032-06-6 (acid-free paper)
    1. Twain, Mark, 1835–1910—Quotations.   2. United
States—Politics and government—Quotations, maxims,
etc.   3. United States—Politics and government—Humor.
4. Political science—Quotations, maxims, etc.   5. Political
science—Humor. I. Hodge, David, 1954–. II. Freeman,
Stacey, 1958–. III. Title. IV. Series.
PS1303.H54   1992
818'.402—dc20   92-14931
                                                 CIP

First printing, November 1992
ISBN: 1-880032-06-6
Printed in the U.S.A. on acid-free paper

For Caleb

It is my conviction that the human race is no proper target for harsh words and bitter criticisms, and that the only justifiable feeling toward it is compassion; it did not invent itself, and it had nothing to do with the planning of its weak and foolish character.

MARK TWAIN'S AUTOBIOGRAPHY

Contents

PUBLISHER'S PREFACE   xi

INTRODUCTION   xiii

CHAPTER 1   Politics, Politicians, and
Parties   1

CHAPTER 2   Patriotism and War   29

CHAPTER 3   Racism and Imperialism   55

CHAPTER 4   Religion   61

CHAPTER 5   Conformity and Progress   73

CHAPTER 6   Morality and Truth   105

ABOUT THE AUTHOR   119

BIBLIOGRAPHIC NOTES   121

ABOUT THE EDITORS   125

Publisher's Preface

Life is an endless cycle of change. We and our world will never remain the same.

Every generation has difficulty relating to the previous generation; even the language changes. The child speaks a different language than the parent does.

It seems almost miraculous, then, that certain voices, certain books, are able to speak not only to one, but to many generations beyond them. The plays and poems of William Shakespeare are still relevant today—still capable of giving us goose bumps, still entertaining, disturbing, and profound. Shakespeare is the writer who, in the English language, defines the word *classic*.

There are many other writers and thinkers who, for a great many reasons, can be considered classic, for they withstand the test of time. We want to present the best of them to you in the New World Library Classic Wisdom Collection. Even though these writers and thinkers lived many years ago, they are still relevant and important in today's world for the enduring words of wisdom they created, words that should forever be kept in print.

Shakti Gawain
Marc Allen
New World Library

Introduction

1992 marks a particularly timely moment for a collection of Twain's political wisdom. In a presidential election year, the flaws and excesses of our political process come into sharper focus. Election years also provide us—for better or worse—the opportunity to reassess our country and its position in the world. More strikingly than at any time in the recent past, we see economic depression, corporate graft and corruption, the ineffectualness of our political leaders, and the inability of government to come to terms with the pressing issues of the day: drug abuse, homelessness, health care, poverty.

Our world becomes increasingly politicized. Despite the end of the Cold War and movement toward global nuclear disarmament, the last five years have witnessed a rash of conventional imperialistic and nationalistic wars: the U.S. invasions of Granada, Panama, and Iraq, the bombing of Libya, the Soviets in Afghanistan, the violent and bloody disintegration of the Yugoslavian and

Soviet federations, and the conflicts throughout the Middle East.

Our problems were not Twain's problems. Politics in the 1990s seems somehow more complex than a century ago. And yet for Twain, the 1890s were a period of transition, and of frustration, as well. He witnessed the transformation of the United States from a simple republic into an imperialistic, capitalistic global aggressor. Twain found much to lament in the "Manifest Destiny" that led the United States to "liberate" native populations in the Philippines, Puerto Rico, and Cuba, and in the hypocrisy lurking behind Christian missionary work in China. He was a bitter foe of monarchy everywhere. Above all, he fought the pretense and dishonesty which had come to be so characteristic of politics in America.

Our definition of "political" is intentionally broad. We believe that Twain's ideas on religion, morality—indeed, on the human race itself—are *inherently* political. Mark Twain spoke and wrote about a great many subjects, and to have limited our selection to the overtly political topics such as Congress or voting or politicians would have meant ignoring a wealth of delightful and thought-provoking commentary.

In many of the speeches, letters, and essays we have left Twain's references to contemporary people and events intact, feeling that this historical dimension enhances the material. It is striking how often, by simply changing names or dates, the material applies to the present, how relevant Twain is a century later.

Even today, controversy surrounds Twain and his writings. Many of his early polemical social critiques appeared in pamphlet form and enjoyed widespread popular success. Yet the critics of his day denigrated Twain because of that very appeal to a mass audience. How ironic then, that pamphlets such as Twain's "War Prayer" spoke so eloquently to the student movement and the New Left in the 1960s, and elevated Twain to the status of a popular hero all over again. It would seem that the 1990s are sorely in need of such time-honored wisdom—despite the fact that Twain's books are still being banned in some parts of the United States today.

As Mark Twain said, "Humor is the good-natured side of any truth." He has been likened to Cervantes and to Shakespeare for his uncanny ability to turn despair into comedy, evil into parody, fury into laughter. Like all great bards, he can show us the absurdity of the human condition, and offer a bit of redemption from the evil that surrounds us.

For, above all else, Mark Twain teaches us that

we are the evil that surrounds us. When he attacks the legislature, or criticizes the politician, he is commenting on himself—on all of us. The mirror he held up to society then, can be held up to us now. If he were alive today, it is certain he would have much to say about the state of things. But why should he repeat himself? Twain's humor—and his truth—transcend his time.

David Hodge
Stacey Freeman

The Political Tales and Truth of
Mark Twain

1

Politics, Politicians, and Parties

Yes, you are right—I am a moralist in disguise; it gets me into heaps of trouble when I go thrashing around in political questions.

Letter to Helene Picard,
MARK TWAIN'S LETTERS (February 22, 1902)

History has tried hard to teach us that we can't have good government under politicians. Now, to go and stick one at the very head of the government couldn't be wise.

NEW YORK HERALD (August 26, 1876)

I asked Tom if countries always apologized when they had done wrong, and he says—"Yes; the little ones does."

TOM SAWYER ABROAD, Chapter XII

I guess the government that robs its own people earns the future it is preparing for itself.

MARK TWAIN: A BIOGRAPHY,
Chapter CCLXXXVI

Wm Penn achieved the deathless gratitude of the savages by merely dealing in a square way with them—well, kind of a square way, anyhow—more rectangular than the *savage* was used to, at any rate. He bought the whole State of Pa from them & paid for it like a man. Paid $40 worth of glass beads & a couple of second-hand blankets. Bought the whole State for that. Why you can't buy its *legislature* for twice the money now.

MARK TWAIN'S NOTEBOOKS AND JOURNALS
(August 1890–June 1891)

THE TEMPERANCE CRUSADE
AND WOMAN'S RIGHTS

The present crusade will doubtless do but little work against intemperance that will be really permanent, but it will do what is as much, or even more, to the purpose, I think. I think it will suggest to more than one man that if women could vote they would vote on the side of morality, even if they did vote and speak rather frantically and furiously; and it will also suggest that when the women once made up their minds that it was not good to leave the all-powerful "primaries" in the hands of loafers, thieves, and pernicious little politicians, they would not sit indolently at home as their husbands and brothers do now, but would hoist their praying banners, take the field in force, pray the assembled political scum back to the holes and slums where they belong, and set up some candidates fit for decent human beings to vote for.

I dearly want the women to be raised to the political altitude of the negro, the imported savage, and the pardoned thief, and allowed to vote. It is our last chance, I think. . . . Both the great parties have failed. I wish we might have a woman's party now, and see how that would work. I feel persuaded that in extending the suffrage to women this country could lose absolutely nothing and

3

might gain a great deal. For thirty centuries history has been iterating and reiterating that in a moral fight woman is simply dauntless, and we all know, even with our eyes shut upon Congress and our voters, that from the day that Adam ate of the apple and told on Eve down to the present day, man, in a moral fight, has pretty uniformly shown himself to be an arrant coward.

EUROPE AND ELSEWHERE (1873)

Mr. Dilworthy appeared in his place in the Senate and offered a resolution appointing a committee to investigate his case. It carried, of course, and the committee was appointed. Straightway the newspapers said:

> Under the guise of appointing a committee to investigate the late Mr. Dilworthy, the Senate yesterday appointed a committee to *investigate his accuser, Mr. Noble*. This is the exact spirit and meaning of the resolution, and the committee cannot try anybody but Mr. Noble without overstepping its authority. That Mr. Dilworthy had the effrontery to offer such a resolution will surprise no one; and that the Senate could entertain it without blushing and pass it without shame will surprise no one. We are now reminded of a note which we have

received from the notorious burglar Murphy,
in which he finds fault with a statement of ours
to the effect that he had served one term in the
penitentiary and also one in the U.S. Senate.
He says, "The latter statement is untrue and
does me great injustice." After an unconscious
sarcasm like that, further comment is
unnecessary.

THE GILDED AGE, Chapter LIX

Our Congresses consist of Christians. In their private life they are true to every obligation of honor;
yet in every session they violate them all, and do it
without shame; because honor to party is above
honor to themselves. It is an accepted law of public
life that in it a man may soil his honor in the interest of party expediency—*must* do it when party
expediency requires it. In private life those men
would bitterly resent—and justly—any insinua-
tion that it would not be safe to leave unwatched
money within their reach; yet you could not
wound their feelings by reminding them that
every time they vote ten dollars to the pension ap-
propriation, nine of it is stolen money and they the
marauders. They have filched the money to take
care of the party; they believe it was right to do it,
they do not see how their private honor is affected;

therefore their consciences are clear and at rest. By vote they do wrongful things every day, in the party interest, which they could not be persuaded to do in private life. In the interest of party expediency they give solemn pledges, they make solemn compacts; in the interest of party expediency they repudiate them without a blush. They would not dream of committing these strange crimes in private life.

CHRISTIAN SCIENCE, Conclusion

But no, that would be common sense—and out of place in a government.

FOLLOWING THE EQUATOR, Chapter XXXI

Political parties who accuse the one in power of gobbling the spoils etc. are like the wolf who looked in at the door and saw the shepherds eating mutton, and said:

"Oh, certainly—it's all right as long as it's you—but there'd be hell to pay if I was to do that."

MARK TWAIN'S NOTEBOOK, Chapter XII

It could probably be shown by facts and figures that there is no distinctly native American criminal class except Congress.

> *Pudd'nhead Wilson's New Calendar,*
> FOLLOWING THE EQUATOR, Chapter VIII

Philip looked at Alice to see if she was in earnest and not chaffing him. Her face was quite sober. Alice was one of those patriotic women in the rural districts, who think men are still selected for Congress on account of qualifications for the office.

"No," said Philip, "the chances are that a man cannot get into Congress now without resorting to arts and means that should render him unfit to go there; of course, there are exceptions; but do you know that I could not go into politics if I were a lawyer, without losing standing somewhat in my profession, and without raising at least a suspicion of my intentions and unselfishness? Why, it is telegraphed all over the country and commented on as something wonderful if a Congressman votes honestly and unselfishly and refuses to take advantage of his position to steal from the government."

"But," insisted Alice, "I should think it a noble ambition to go to Congress, if it is so bad, and help reform it. I don't believe it is as corrupt as the English parliament used to be, if there is any truth in the novels, and I suppose that is reformed."

"I'm sure I don't know where the reform is to begin. I've seen a perfectly capable, honest man, time and again, run against an illiterate trickster, and get beaten. I suppose if the people wanted decent members of Congress they would elect them. Perhaps," continued Philip with a smile, "the women will have to vote."

"Well, I should be willing to, if it were a necessity, just as I would go to war and do what I could, if the country couldn't be saved otherwise," said Alice, with a spirit that surprised Philip, well as he thought he knew her. "If I were a young gentleman in these times—"

Philip laughed outright. "It's just what Ruth used to say, 'if she were a man.' I wonder if all the young ladies are contemplating a change of sex."

"No, only a changed sex," retorted Alice. "We contemplate for the most part young men who don't care for anything they ought to care for."

"Well," said Philip, looking humble, "I care for some things, you and Ruth for instance; perhaps I ought not to. Perhaps I ought to care for Congress and that sort of thing."

THE GILDED AGE, Chapter L

"I think Congress always tries to do as near right as it can, according to its lights. A man can't ask any fairer than that. The first preliminary it always starts out on, is to clean itself, so to speak. It will arraign two or three dozen of its members, or maybe four or five dozen, for taking bribes to vote for this and that and the other bill last winter."

"It goes up into the dozens, does it?"

"Well, yes; in a free country like ours, where any man can run for Congress and anybody can vote for him, you can't expect immortal purity all the time—it ain't in nature. Sixty or eighty of a hundred and fifty people are bound to get in who are not angels in disguise . . . but still it is a very good average; very good indeed. As long as it averages as well as that, I think we can feel very well satisfied. Even in these days, when people growl so much and the newspapers are so out of patience, there is still a very respectable minority of honest men in Congress."

THE GILDED AGE, Chapter LI

Those burglars that broke into my house recently are in jail, and if they keep on they will go to Congress. When a person starts downhill you can never tell where he's going to stop.

> MARK TWAIN: A BIOGRAPHY,
> Chapter CCLXXIV

All Congresses and Parliaments have a kindly feeling for idiots, and a compassion for them, on account of personal experience and heredity.

> MARK TWAIN IN ERUPTION
> (November 24, 1906)

Bill Styles, lobbying in behalf of a candidate for U.S. Senator—in the legislature—spoke of the low grade of legislative morals, "kind of discouragin', you see, it's so hard to find men of so high type of morals that they'll *stay* bought."

> MARK TWAIN'S NOTEBOOK, Chapter XX

I had heard so much about the celebrated fortune-teller Madame—that I went to see her yesterday.

". . . Yours was not, in the beginning, a criminal nature, but circumstances changed it. At the age of nine you stole sugar. At the age of fifteen you stole money. At twenty you stole horses. At twenty-five you committed arson. At thirty, hardened in crime, you became an editor. You are now a public lecturer. Worse things are in store for you. You will be sent to Congress. Next, to the penitentiary. Finally, happiness will come again—all will be well—you will be hanged."

I was now in tears. It seemed hard enough to go to Congress; but to be hanged—this was too sad, too dreadful. The woman seemed surprised at my grief.

"Lionizing Murderers,"
SKETCHES NEW AND OLD

There are some natures which never grow large enough to speak out and say a bad act *is* a bad act, until they have inquired into the politics or the nationality of the man who did it . . . Cain is branded a murderer so heartily and unanimously in America, only because he was neither a Democrat nor a Republican.

"Memoranda," GALAXY MAGAZINE
(May 1870)

Reader, suppose you were an idiot. And suppose you were a member of Congress. But I repeat myself.

MARK TWAIN: A BIOGRAPHY,
Chapter CXXXVIII

It is the will of God that we must have critics, and missionaries, and congressmen, and humorists, and we must bear the burden.

MARK TWAIN'S AUTOBIOGRAPHY
(February 7, 1906)

I have often wondered at the condition of things which set aside morality in politics and make possible the election of men whose unfitness is apparent. A mother will teach her boy at her knee to tell the truth, to be kind, to avoid all that is immoral. She will painstakingly guide his thoughts and actions so that he may grow up possessed of all the manly virtues, and the father of that boy will, when it comes time for his son to cast his first vote, take him aside and advise him to vote for a bad man who is on the Democratic ticket because he has always adhered to Democratic principles. Could anything be more absurd?

NEW YORK HERALD (November 12, 1905)

The radical of one century is the conservative of the next. The radical invents the views. When he has worn them out the conservative adopts them.

MARK TWAIN'S NOTEBOOK, Chapter XXXI

I think I can say, and say with pride, that we have some legislatures that bring higher prices than any in the world.

MARK TWAIN'S SPEECHES (July 4, 1872)

Congressman is the trivialest distinction for a full-grown man.

MARK TWAIN'S NOTEBOOK, Chapter XIII

If we would learn what the human race really *is* at bottom, we need only observe it in election times. A Hartford clergyman met me in the street and spoke of a new nominee—denounced the nomination, in strong, earnest words—words that were refreshing for their independence, their manliness. He said, "I ought to be proud, perhaps, for this nominee is a relative of mine; on the contrary, I am humiliated and disgusted, for I know him intimately—familiarly—and I know that he is an unscrupulous scoundrel, and always has been." You should have seen this clergyman preside at a political meeting forty days later, and urge, and plead, and gush—and you should have heard him paint the character of this same nominee. You would have supposed he was describing the Cid, and Greatheart, and Sir Galahad, and Bayard the Spotless all rolled into one. Was he sincere? Yes— by that time; and therein lies the pathos of it all, the hopelessness of it all. It shows at what trivial cost of effort a man can teach himself to lie, and learn to believe it, when he perceives, by the general drift, that that is the popular thing to do. Does he believe his lie *yet?* Oh, probably not; he has no further use for it. It was but a passing incident; he spared to it the moment that was its due, then hastened back to the serious business of his life.

MARK TWAIN'S AUTOBIOGRAPHY
(January 23, 1906)

A pretty air in an opera is prettier there than it could be anywhere else, I suppose, just as an honest man in politics shines more than he would elsewhere.

A TRAMP ABROAD, Chapter IX

Kings are but the hampered servants of parliament and the people; parliaments sit in chains forged by their constituency; the editor of a newspaper cannot be independent, but must work with one hand tied behind him by party and patrons, and be content to utter only half or two-thirds of his mind; no clergyman is a free man and may speak the whole truth, regardless of his parish's opinions; writers of all kinds are manacled servants of the public. We write frankly and fearlessly, but then we "modify" before we print. In truth, every man, woman, and child has a master, and worries, and frets in servitude.

LIFE ON THE MISSISSIPPI, Chapter XIV

If you know a man's nationality you can come within a split hair of guessing the complexion of his religion: English—Protestant; American— ditto; Spaniard, Frenchman, Irishman, Italian,

South American, Austrian—Roman Catholic; Russian—Greek Catholic; Turk—Mohammedan; and so on. And when you know the man's religious complexion, you know what sort of religious books he reads when he wants some more light, and what sort of books he avoids, lest by accident he get more light than he wants. In America if you know which party-collar a voter wears, you know what his associations are, and how he came by his politics, and which breed of newspaper he reads to get light, and which breed he diligently avoids, and which breed of mass meetings he attends in order to broaden his political knowledge, and which breed of mass meetings he doesn't attend, except to refute its doctrines with brickbats.

WHAT IS MAN?, Chapter IV

I cannot understand the philosophy of the man who, looked up to as a model citizen, loses sight of the morality of politics when it comes to casting his ballot. Why, it's nothing but a question of morality. And I know lots of men who will throw aside all considerations of morality when they go to the polls, and will vote for the man nominated by his party irrespective of his personal fitness for the place.

NEW YORK HERALD (November 12, 1905)

We are discreet sheep; we wait to see how the drove is going, and then go with the drove. We have two opinions; one private, which we are afraid to express; and another one—the one we use—which we force ourselves to wear to please Mrs. Grundy, until habit makes us comfortable in it, and the custom of defending it presently makes us love it, adore it, and forget how pitifully we came by it. Look at it in politics. Look at the candidates whom we loathe one year, and are afraid to vote against the next; whom we cover with unimaginable filth one year, and fall down on the public platform and worship the next—and keep on doing it until the habitual shutting of our eyes to last year's evidences brings us presently to a sincere and stupid belief in this year's. Look at the tyranny of party—at what is called party allegiance, party loyalty—a snare invented by designing men for selfish purposes—and which turns voters into chattels, slaves, rabbits, and all the while their masters, and they themselves are shouting rubbish about liberty, independence, freedom of opinion, freedom of speech, honestly unconscious of the fantastic contradiction; and forgetting or ignoring that their fathers and the churches shouted the same blasphemies a generation earlier when they were closing their doors against the hunted slave, beating his handful of humane defenders with Bible texts and billies, and pocketing the insults and licking the shoes of his Southern master.

> "The Character of Man,"
> MARK TWAIN'S AUTOBIOGRAPHY,
> Vol. II (January 23, 1906)

A Tribute

[A mock speech written after the election of Grover Cleveland]

Mr. Chairman,

That is a noble and beautiful ancient sentiment which admonishes us to speak well of the dead. Therefore let us try to do this for our late friend who is mentioned in the text. How full of life and strength and confidence and pride he was but a few short months ago; and, alas! how dead he is to-day! We that are gathered at these obsequies, we that are here to bury this dust, and sing the parting hymn, and say the comforting word to the widow and the orphan now left destitute and sorrowing by him, their support and stay in the post office, the consulship, the navy yard, and the Indian reservation—we knew him, right well and familiarly we knew him; and so it is meet that we, and not strangers, should take upon ourselves these last offices, lest his reputation suffer through explanations of him which might not explain him happily, and justifications of him which might not justify him conclusively. First, it is right and well that we censure him, in those few minor details wherein some slight censure may seem to be demanded; to the end that when we come to speak his praises the good he did may shine with all the more intolerable brightness by the contrast.

To begin, then, with the twilight side of his character: He was a slave; not a turbulent and troublesome, but a meek and docile, cringing and fawning, dirt-eating and dirt-prefering slave; and Party was his lord and master. He had no mind of his own, no will of his own, no opinion of his own; body and soul he was the property and chattel of that master, to be bought and sold, bartered, traded, *given* away, at his nod and beck—branded, mutilated, boiled in oil, if need were. And the desire of his heart was to make of a nation of freemen a nation of slaves like to himself; to bring to pass a time when it might be said that "all are for the Party, and none are for the State;" and the labors of his diligent hand and brain did finally compass his desire. For he fooled the people with plausible new readings of familiar old principles, and beguiled them to the degradation of their manhood and the destruction of their liberties. He taught them that the only true freedom of thought is to think as the party thinks; that the only true freedom of speech is to speak as the party dictates; that the only righteous toleration is toleration of what the party approves; that patriotism, duty, citizenship, devotion to country, loyalty to the flag, are all summed up in loyalty to party. Save the party, uphold the party, make the party victorious, though all things else go to ruin and the grave.

In these few little things he who lies here cold in death was faulty. Say we no more concerning them, but over them draw the veil of a charitable oblivion; for the good which he did far overpasses this little evil. With grateful hearts we may unite in praises and thanksgiving to him for one majestic fact of his life—that in his zeal for his cause he finally overdid it. The precious result was that a change came; and that change remains, and will endure, and on its banner is written—

"Not all are for the Party—*now* some are for the State."

MARK TWAIN'S SPEECHES (1884)

One of the first and most startling things you find out is, that every individual you encounter in the city of Washington almost—and certainly every separate and distinct individual in the public em-

ployment, from the highest bureau chief, clear
down to the maid who scrubs Department halls, the
night watchmen of the public buildings, and the
. . . [man] who purifies the Department spit-
toons—represents Political Influence. Unless you
can get the ear of a Senator, or a Congressman, or a
Chief of a Bureau or Department, and persuade
him to use his "influence" in your behalf, you cannot get an employment of the most trivial nature in
Washington. Mere merit, fitness, and capability,
are useless baggage to you without "influence."
The population of Washington consists pretty
much entirely of government employés and the
people who board them. There are thousands of
these employés, and they have gathered there from
every corner of the Union and got their berths
through the intercession (command is nearer the
word) of Senators and Representatives of their re-
spective States. It would be an odd circumstance to
see a girl get employment at three or four dollars a
week in one of the great public cribs without any
political grandee to back her, but merely because
she was worthy, and competent, and a good citizen
of a free country that "treats all persons alike."
Washington would be mildly thunderstruck at such
a thing as that. If you are a member of Congress (no
offense), and one of your constituents who doesn't
know anything, and does not want to go into the
bother of learning something, and has no money,

and no employment, and can't earn a living, comes besieging you for help, do you say, "Come, my friend, if your services were valuable you could get employment elsewhere—don't want you here"? Oh, no. You take him to a Department and say, "Here, give this person something to pass away the time at—and a salary"—and the thing is done. You throw him on his country. He is his country's child, let his country support him. There is something good and motherly about Washington, the grand old benevolent National Asylum for the Helpless.

THE GILDED AGE, Chapter XXIV

We will not hire a blacksmith who never lifted a sledge. We will not hire a school-teacher who does not know the alphabet. We will not have a man about us in our business life, in any walk of it, low or high, unless he has served an apprenticeship and can prove that he is capable of doing the work he offers to do. We even require a plumber to know something about his business, that he shall at least know which side of a pipe is the inside. But when you come to our civil service, we serenely fill great numbers of our minor public offices with ignoramuses.

NEW YORK TIMES (October 2, 1876)

Principles is another name for prejudices. I have no prejudices in politics, religion, literature, or anything else.

I am now on my way to my own country to run for the presidency because there are not yet enough candidates in the field, and those who have entered are too much hampered by their own principles, which are prejudices.

I propose to go there to purify the political atmosphere. I am in favor of everything everybody is in favor of. What you should do is to satisfy the whole nation, not half of it, for then you would only be half a President.

There could not be a broader platform than mine. I am in favor of anything and everything— of temperance and intemperance, morality and qualified immorality, gold standard and free silver.

I have tried all sorts of things, and that is why I want to try the great position of ruler of a country. I have been in turn reporter, editor, publisher, author, lawyer, burglar. I have worked my way up, and wish to continue to do so.

MARK TWAIN'S SPEECHES (May 4, 1900)

The coat of arms of the human race ought to consist of a man with an ax on his shoulder proceeding toward a grindstone, or it ought to represent the several members of the human race holding out the hat to one another; for we are all beggars, each in his own way. One beggar is too proud to beg for pennies, but will beg for an introduction into society; another does not care for society, but he wants a postmastership; another will inveigle a lawyer into conversation and then sponge on him for free advice. The man who wouldn't do any of these things will beg for the Presidency. Each admires his own dignity and greatly guards it, but in his opinion the others haven't any.

MARK TWAIN: A BIOGRAPHY, Chapter CCLXII

"They've been learnt to do all sorts of hard and troublesome things. S'pose you could cultivate a flea up to the size of a man, and keep his natural smartness a-growing and a-growing right along up, bigger and bigger, and keener and keener, in the same proportion—where'd the human race be, do you reckon? That flea would be President of the United States, and you couldn't any more prevent it than you can prevent lightning."

TOM SAWYER ABROAD, Chapter VII

I miss a good many faces. They have gone—gone to the tomb, to the gallows, or to the White House. All of us are entitled to at least one of these distinctions, and it behooves us to be wise and prepare for all.

MARK TWAIN: A BIOGRAPHY, Chapter CLII

The principal editorial comment in *Collier's Weekly* for July 11th [1908] contains seven or eight sentences—short ones, therefore it is a brief paragraph. It is a wonderful accumulation of rubbish to be packed into so small a space. It is a burst of servile and insane admiration and adulation of President Roosevelt. It purports to be a reflection of the sentiment of the nation; that is to say, the Republican bulk of the nation. It ought to grieve me to concede that it does reflect the sentiment of the Republican bulk of the nation, but it doesn't. To my mind, the bulk of any nation's opinion about its president, or its king, or its emperor, or its politics, or its religion, is without value and not worth weighing or considering or examining. There is nothing mental in it; it is all feeling, and procured at secondhand without any assistance from the proprietor's reasoning powers.

On the other hand, it would grieve me deeply to be obliged to believe that any very large number of sane and thinking and intelligent Republicans privately admire Mr. Roosevelt and do not despise him. Publicly, all sane and intelligent Republicans worship Mr. Roosevelt and would not dare to do otherwise where any considerable company of listeners was present; and this is quite natural, since sane and intelligent human beings are like all other human beings, and carefully and cautiously and diligently conceal their private real opinions from the world and give out fictitious ones in their stead for general consumption.

MARK TWAIN IN ERUPTION (July 14, 1908)

Does the human being reason? No; he thinks, muses, reflects, but doesn't reason. Thinks *about* a thing; rehearses its statistics and its parts and applies to them what other people on his side of the question have said about them, but he does not compare the part himself, and is not capable of doing it.

That is, in the two things which are the peculiar domain of the heart, not the mind—politics and religion. He doesn't want to know the other side. He wants arguments and statistics for his own side, and nothing more.

MARK TWAIN'S NOTEBOOK, Chapter XXVII

I am quite sure now that often, very often, in matters concerning religion and politics a man's reasoning powers are not above the monkey's.

"The Holy Grail," MARK TWAIN IN ERUPTION

Elmira, Sept. 17, '84

My Dear Howells,

Somehow I can't seem to rest quiet under the idea of your voting for Blaine. I believe you said something about the country and the party. Certainly allegiance to these is well, but as certainly a man's *first* duty is to his own conscience and honor. The party of the country come second to that, and never first. I don't ask you to vote *at all*— I only urge you to not soil yourself by voting for Blaine.

When you wrote before, you were able to say the charges against him were not proven. But you know now that they are proven, and it seems to me that that bars you and all other honest and honorable men (who are independently situated) from voting for him.

It is not necessary to vote for Cleveland; the only necessary thing to do, as I understand it, is that a man shall keep *himself* clean (by withholding his vote for an improper man) even though the party and the country go to destruction in consequence. It is not *parties* that make or save countries or that build them to greatness—it is clean men, clean ordinary citizens, rank and file, the masses. Clean masses are not made by individuals standing back till the rest become clean.

As I said before, I think a man's first duty is to his own honor, not to his country and not to his party. Don't be offended; I mean no offence. I am not so concerned about the *rest* of the nation, but—well, good-bye.

Letter to William Dean Howells,
MARK TWAIN'S LETTERS (September 17, 1884)

I will not go any further into politics as I would get excited, and I don't like to get excited.

NEW YORK TIMES (March 17, 1901)

2

Patriotism and War

PEACE WITH HONOR
[Mark Twain on the Philippine War]

I pray you to pause and consider. Against our traditions we are now entering upon an unjust and trivial war, a war against a helpless people, and for a base object—robbery. At first our citizens spoke out against this thing by an impulse natural to their training. Today they have turned, and their voice is the other way. What caused this change? Merely a politician's trick—a high-sounding phrase, a blood-stirring phrase which turned their uncritical heads: *Our Country, right or wrong!* An empty phrase, a silly phrase. It was shouted by every newspaper, it was thundered from the pulpit, the Superintendent of Public Instruction placarded it in every schoolhouse in the land, the War Department inscribed it upon the flag. And every man who failed to shout it, or who was silent, was proclaimed a traitor—none but those others were patriots. To be a patriot, one had to say, and keep on saying, "Our Country, right or wrong," and urge on the little war. Have you not perceived that phrase is an insult to the nation. . . .

Only when a republic's *life* is in danger should a man uphold his government when it is in the wrong. There is no other time.

This Republic's life is not in peril. The nation has sold its honor for a phrase. It has swung itself loose from its safe anchorage and is drifting, its helm is in pirate hands. The stupid phrase needed help, and it got another one: "Even if the war be wrong we are in it and must fight it out: *we cannot retire from it without dishonor.*" Why, not even a burglar could have said it better. We cannot withdraw from this sordid raid because to grant peace to those little people upon their terms—independence—would dishonor us. You have flung away Adam's phrase—you should take it up and examine it again. He said, *"An inglorious peace is better than a dishonorable war."*

You have planted a seed, and it will grow.

MARK TWAIN AND THE THREE R'S

THE WAR PRAYER

It was a time of great and exalting excitement. The country was up in arms, the war was on, in every breast burned the holy fire of patriotism; the drums were beating, the bands playing, the toy pistols popping, the bunched firecrackers hissing and spluttering; on every hand and far down the receding and fading spread of roofs and balconies a fluttering wilderness of flags flashed in the sun; daily the young volunteers marched down the wide avenue gay and fine in their new uniforms, the proud fathers and mothers and sisters and sweethearts cheering them with voices choked with happy emotion as they swung by; nightly the packed mass meetings listened, panting, to patriot oratory which stirred the deepest deeps of their hearts, and which they interrupted at briefest intervals with cyclones of applause, the tears running down their cheeks the while; in the churches the pastors preached devotion to flag and country, and invoked the God of Battles, beseeching His aid in our good cause in outpourings of fervid eloquence which moved every listener. It was indeed a glad and gracious time, and the half dozen rash spirits that ventured to disapprove of the war and cast a doubt upon its righteousness straightway got such a stern and angry warning that for their personal safety's sake they quickly shrank out of sight and offended no more in that way.

Sunday morning came—next day the battalions would leave for the front; the church was filled; the volunteers were there, their young faces alight with martial dreams—visions of the stern advance, the gathering momentum, the rushing charge, the flashing sabers, the flight of the foe, the tumult, the enveloping smoke, the fierce pursuit, the surrender!—then home from the war, bronzed heroes, welcomed, adored, submerged in golden seas of glory! With the volunteers sat their dear ones, proud, happy, and envied by the neighbors and friends who had no sons and brothers to send forth to the field of honor, there to win for the flag, or, failing, die the noblest of noble deaths. The service proceeded; a war chapter from the Old Testament was read; the first prayer was said; it was followed by an organ burst that shook the building, and with one impulse the house rose, with glowing eyes and beating hearts, and poured out that tremendous invocation—"God the all-terrible! Thou who ordainest, Thunder thy clarion and lightning thy sword!" Then came the "long" prayer. None could remember the like of it for passionate pleading and moving and beautiful language. The burden of its supplication was, that an ever-merciful and benignant Father of us all would watch over our noble young soldiers, and aid, comfort, and encourage them in their patriotic work; bless them, shield them in the day of battle and the hour of peril, bear them in His mighty hand, make them strong and confident, invincible in the bloody onset; help them to crush the foe, grant to them and to their flag and country imperishable honor and glory—

An aged stranger entered and moved with slow and noiseless step up the main aisle, his eyes fixed upon the minister, his long body clothed in a robe that reached to his feet, his head bare, his white hair descending in a frothy cataract to his shoulders, his seamy face unnaturally pale, pale even to ghastliness. With all eyes following him and wondering, he made his silent way; without pausing, he ascended to the preacher's side and stood there, waiting. With shut lids the preacher, unconscious of his presence, continued his moving prayer, and at last finished it with the words, uttered in fervent appeal, "Bless our arms, grant us the victory, O Lord our God, Father and Protector of our land and flag!"

The stranger touched his arm, motioned him to step aside—which the startled minister did—and took his place. During some moments he surveyed the spellbound audience with solemn eyes, in which burned an uncanny light; then in a deep voice he said:

"I come from the Throne—bearing a message from Almighty God!" The words smote the house with a shock; if the stranger perceived it he gave no attention. "He has heard the prayer of His servant your shepherd, and will grant it if such shall be your desire after I, His messenger, shall have explained to you its import—that is to say, its full import. For it is like unto many of the prayers of men, in that it asks for more than he who utters it is aware of—except he pause and think.

"God's servant and yours has prayed his prayer. Has he paused and taken thought? Is it one prayer? No, it is two—one uttered, the other not. Both have reached the ear of Him Who heareth all supplications, the spoken and the unspoken. Ponder this—keep it in mind. If you would beseech a blessing upon yourself, beware! lest without intent you invoke a curse upon a neighbor at the same time. If you pray for the blessing of rain upon your crop which needs it, by that act you are possibly praying for a curse upon some neighbor's crop which may not need rain and can be injured by it.

"You have heard your servant's prayer—the uttered part of it. I am commissioned of God to put into words the other part of it—that part which the pastor—and also you in your hearts—fervently prayed silently. And ignorantly and unthinkingly? God grant that it was so! You heard these words: 'Grant us the victory, O Lord our

God!' That is sufficient. The *whole* of the uttered prayer is compact into those pregnant words. Elaborations were not necessary. When you have prayed for victory, you have prayed for many unmentioned results which follow victory—*must* follow it, cannot help but follow it. Upon the listening spirit of God the Father fell also the unspoken part of the prayer. He commandeth me to put it into words. Listen!

"O Lord our Father, our young patriots, idols of our hearts, go forth to battle—be Thou near them! With them—in spirit—we also go forth from the sweet peace of our beloved firesides to smite the foe. O Lord our God, help us to tear their soldiers to bloody shreds with our shells; help us to cover their smiling fields with the pale forms of their patriot dead; help us to drown the thunder of the guns with the shrieks of their wounded, writhing in pain; help us to lay waste their humble homes with a hurricane of fire; help us to wring the hearts of their unoffending widows with unavailing grief; help us to turn them out roofless with their little children to wander unfriended the wastes of their desolated land in rages and hunger and thirst, sports of the sun flames of summer and the icy winds of winter, broken in spirit, worn with travail, imploring Thee for the refuge of the grave and denied it—for our sakes who adore Thee, Lord, blast their hopes, blight their lives, protract their bitter pilgrimage, make heavy their steps, water their way with their tears, stain the white snow with the blood of their wounded feet! We ask it, in the spirit of love, of Him Who is the Source of Love, and Who is the ever-faithful refuge and friend of all that are sore beset and seek His aid with humble and contrite hearts. Amen."

(*After a pause.*) "Ye have prayed it; if ye still desire it, speak! The messenger of the Most High waits."

It was believed afterward that the man was a lunatic, because there was no sense in what he said.

EUROPE AND ELSEWHERE (1904–5)

A man can be a Christian *or* a patriot, but he can't legally be a Christian *and* a patriot—except in the usual way: one of the two with the mouth, the other with the heart. The spirit of Christianity proclaims the brotherhood of the race and the meaning of that strong word has not been left to guesswork, but made tremendously definite—the Christian must forgive his brother man all crimes he can imagine and commit, and all insults he can conceive and utter—forgive these injuries how many times?—seventy times seven—another way of saying there shall be no limit to this forgiveness. That is the spirit and the law of Christianity. Well—patriotism has *its* law. And it also is a perfectly definite one, there are no vaguenesses about it. It commands that the brother over the border shall be sharply watched and brought to book every time he does us a hurt or offends us with an insult. Word it as softly as you please, the spirit of patriotism is the spirit of the dog and the wolf. The moment there is a misunderstanding about a boundary line or a hamper of fish or some other squalid matter, see patriotism rise, and hear him split the universe with his war-whoop. The spirit of patriotism being in its nature jealous and selfish, is just in man's line, it comes natural to him—he can live up to all its requirements to the letter; but the spirit of Christianity is not in its entirety possible to him.

The prayer concealed in what I have been saying is, not that patriotism should cease and not that the talk about universal brotherhood should cease, but that the incongruous firm be dissolved and each limb of it be required to transact business by itself, for the future.

MARK TWAIN'S NOTEBOOK, Chapter XXX

We are the lavishest and showiest and most luxury-loving people on the earth; and at our masthead we fly our one true and honest symbol, the gaudiest flag the world has ever seen.

"Diplomatic Pay and Clothes," FORUM
(March 1899)

And so, by these Providences of God—the phrase is the government's, not mine—we are a World Power; and are glad and proud, and have a back seat in the family. With tacks in it. At least we are letting on to be glad and proud; it is the best way. Indeed, it is the only way. We must maintain our dignity, for people are looking. We are a World Power; we cannot get out of it now, and we must make the best of it.

MARK TWAIN: A BIOGRAPHY, Chapter CCXX

If this nation has ever trusted in God, that time has gone by; for nearly half a century almost its entire trust has been in the Republican party and the dollar—mainly the dollar.

MARK TWAIN IN ERUPTION
(December 2, 1907)

I cannot believe that the prediction will come true, for the reason that prophecies which promise valuable things, desirable things, good things, worthy things, never come true. Prophecies of this kind are like wars fought in a good cause—they are so rare that they don't count.

MARK TWAIN'S AUTOBIOGRAPHY
(March 14, 1906)

And always we had wars, and more wars, and still other wars—all over Europe, all over the world. "Sometimes in the private interest of royal families," Satan said, "sometimes to crush a weak nation; but never a war started by the aggressor for any clean purpose—there is no such war in the history of the race.

"Now," said Satan, "you have seen your progress down to the present, and you must confess that it is wonderful—in its way. We must now exhibit the future."

He showed us slaughters more terrible in their destruction of life, more devastating in their engines of war, than any we had seen.

"You perceive," he said, "that you have made continual progress. Cain did his murder with a club; the Hebrews did their murders with javelins and swords; the Greeks and Romans added protective armor and the fine arts of military organization and generalship; the Christian has added guns and gunpowder; a few centuries from now he will have so greatly improved the deadly effectiveness of his weapons of slaughter that all men will confess that without Christian civilization war must have remained a poor and trifling thing to the end of time."

THE MYSTERIOUS STRANGER, Chapter VIII

"The gospel of peace" is always making a deal of noise, always rejoicing in its progress but always neglecting to furnish statistics. There are no peaceful nations now. All Christendom is a soldier-camp. The poor have been taxed in some nations to the starvation point to support the giant armaments which Christian governments have built up, each to protect itself from the rest of the Christian brotherhood, and incidentally to snatch any scrap of real estate left exposed by a weaker owner. King Leopold II of Belgium, the most intensely Christian monarch, since Alexander VI, that has escaped hell thus far, has stolen an entire kingdom in Africa, and in fourteen years of Christian endeavor there has reduced the population

from thirty millions to fifteen by murder and mu-
tiliation and overwork, confiscating the labor of
the helpless natives, and giving them nothing in
return but salvation and a home in Heaven, furnished at the last moment by the Christian priest.

Within the last generation each Christian
power has turned the bulk of its attention to finding out newer and still newer and more and more
effective ways of killing Christians, and, incidentally, a pagan now and then; and the surest way to
get rich quickly in Christ's earthly kingdom is to
invent a kind of gun that can kill more Christians
at one shot than any other existing kind. All the
Christian nations are at it. The more advanced
they are, the bigger and more destructive engines
of war they create.

MARK TWAIN: A BIOGRAPHY

I now perceive why all men are the deadly and un-
compromising enemies of the rattlesnake: it is
merely because the rattlesnake has not speech.
Monarchy has speech, and by it has been able to
persuade men that it differs somehow from the
rattlesnake, has something valuable about it somewhere, something worth preserving, something
even good and high and fine, when properly "mod-

ified," something entitling it to protection from the club of the first comer who catches it out of its hole. It seems a most strange delusion and not reconcilable with our superstition that a man is a reasoning being. If a house is afire, we reason confidently that it is the first comer's plain duty to put the fire out in any way he can—drown it with water, blow it up with dynamite, use any and all means to stop the spread of the fire and save the rest of the city. What is the Czar of Russia but a house afire in the midst of a city of eighty millions of inhabitants? Yet instead of extinguishing him, together with his nest and system, the liberation-parties are all anxious to merely cool him down a little and keep him.

It seems to me that this is illogical—idiotic, in fact. Suppose you had this granite-hearted, bloody-jawed maniac of Russia loose in your house, chasing the helpless women and little children—your own. What would you do with him, supposing you had a shotgun? Well, he *is* loose in your house—Russia. And with your shotgun in your hand, you stand trying to think up ways to "modify" him.

Do these liberation-parties think that they can succeed in a project which has been attempted a million times in the history of the world and has never in one single instance been successful—the "modification" of a despotism by other means than bloodshed? They seem to think they can. My privilege to write these sanguinary sentences in soft security was bought for me by rivers of blood poured upon many fields, in many lands, but I possess not one single little paltry right or privilege that come to be as a result of petition, persuasion, agitation for reform, or any kindred method of procedure. When we consider that not even the most responsible English monarch ever yielded back a stolen public right until it was wrenched from them by bloody violence, is it rational to suppose that gentler methods can win privileges in Russia?

Letter to the Editor of Free Russia (unpublished)
MARK TWAIN'S LETTERS (1890)

I notice that God is on both sides in this war; thus history repeats itself. But I am the only person who has noticed this; everybody here thinks He is playing the game for this side, and for this side only.

Letter to William Dean Howells,
MARK TWAIN'S LETTERS (January 26, 1900)

There has never been a just one, never an honorable one—on the part of the instigator of the war. I can see a million years ahead, and this rule will never change in so many as half a dozen instances. The loud little handful—as usual—will shout for the war. The pulpit will—warily and cautiously—object—at first; the great, big, dull bulk of the nation will rub its sleepy eyes and try to make out why there should be a war, and will say, earnestly and indignantly, "It is unjust and dishonorable, and there is no necessity for it." Then the handful will shout louder. A few fair men on the other side will argue and reason against the war with speech and pen, and at first will have a hearing and be applauded; but it will not last long; those others will outshout them, and presently the anti-war audiences will thin out and lose popularity. Before long you will see this curious thing: the speakers stoned from the platform, and free speech strangled by hordes of furious men who in their secret hearts are still at one with those stoned speakers—as earlier—but do not dare to say so. And now the whole nation—pulpit and all—will take up the war-cry, and shout itself hoarse, and mob any honest man who ventures to open his mouth; and presently such mouths will cease to open. Next the statesmen will invent cheap lies, putting the blame upon the nation that is attacked, and every man will be glad of those conscience-soothing falsities, and will diligently study them, and refuse to examine any refutations of them; and thus he will by and by convince himself that the war is just, and will thank God for the better sleep he enjoys after this process of grotesque self-deception.

THE MYSTERIOUS STRANGER, Chapter IX

In the North, before the War, the man who opposed slavery was despised and ostracized, and insulted. By the "Patriots." Then, by and by, the "Patriots" went over to his side, and thenceforth his attitude became patriotism.

There are two kinds of patriotism—monarchical patriotism and republican patriotism. In the one case the government and the king may rightfully furnish you their notions of patriotism; in the other, neither the government nor the entire nation is privileged to dictate to any individual what the form of his patriotism shall be. The Gospel of the Monarchical Patriotism is: "The King can do no wrong." We have adopted it with all its servility, with an unimportant change in the wording: "Our country, right *or* wrong!"

We have thrown away the most valuable asset we have—the individual right to oppose both flag and country when he (just *he* by himself) believes them to be in the wrong. We have thrown it away; and with it all that was really respectable about that grotesque and laughable word, Patriotism.

MARK TWAIN'S NOTEBOOK, Chapter XXXV

You see my kind of loyalty was loyalty to one's country, not to its institutions or its officeholders. The country is the real thing, the substantial thing, the eternal thing; it is the thing to watch over, and care for, and be loyal to; institutions are extraneous, they are its mere clothing, and clothing can wear out, become ragged, cease to be comfortable, cease to protect the body from winter, disease, and death. To be loyal to rags, to shout for rags, to worship rags, to die for rags—that is a loyalty of unreason, it is pure animal; it belongs to monarchy; let monarchy keep it. I was from Connecticut, whose Constitution declares "that all political power is inherent in the people, and all free governments are founded on their benefit; and that they have instituted for their benefit; and that they have *at all times* an undeniable and indefeasible right to *alter their form of government* in such a manner as they may think expedient."

Under that gospel, the citizen who thinks he sees that the commonwealth's political clothes are worn out, and yet holds his peace and does not agitate for a new suit, is disloyal; he is a traitor. That he may be the only one who thinks he sees this decay, does not excuse him; it is his duty to agitate anyway, and it is the duty of the others to vote him down if they do not see the matter as he does.

A CONNECTICUT YANKEE IN KING ARTHUR'S
COURT, Chapter XIII

I would teach patriotism in the schools, and teach it this way: I would throw out the old maxim, "My country, right or wrong, &c.," and instead I would say, "My country when she is right."

I would not take my patriotism from my neighbor or from Congress. I should teach the children in the schools that there are certain ideals, and one of them is that all men are created free and equal. Another that the proper government is that which exists by the consent of the governed.

NEW YORK TIMES (March 17, 1901)

47

AS REGARDS PATRIOTISM

It is agreed, in this country, that if a man can arrange his religion so that it perfectly satisfies his conscience, it is not incumbent upon him to care whether the arrangement is satisfactory to anyone else or not.

In Austria and some other countries this is not the case. There the State arranges a man's religion for him, he has no voice in it himself.

Patriotism is merely a religion—love of country, worship of country, devotion to the country's flag and honor and welfare.

In absolute monarchies it is furnished from the throne, cut and dried, to the subject; in England and America it is furnished, cut and dried, to the citizen by the politician and the newspaper.

The newspaper-and-politician-manufactured Patriot often gags in private over his dose; but he takes it, and keeps it on his stomach the best he can. Blessed are the meek.

Sometimes, in the beginning of an insane shabby political upheaval, he is strongly moved to revolt but he doesn't do it—he knows better. He knows that his maker would find out—the maker of his Patriotism, the windy and incoherent six-dollar subeditor of his village newspaper—and would bray out in print and call him a Traitor. And

how dreadful that would be. It makes him tuck his
tail between his legs and shiver. We all know—the
reader knows it quite well—that two or three years
ago nine-tenths of the human tails in England and
America performed just that act. Which is to say,
nine-tenths of the Patriots in England and America
turned traitor to keep from being called traitor.
Isn't it true? You know it to be true. Isn't it
curious?

Yet it was not a thing to be very seriously
ashamed of. A man can seldom—very, very seldom—fight a winning fight against his training;
the odds are too heavy. For many a year—perhaps
always—the training of the two nations had been
dead against independence in political thought,
persistently inhospitable toward Patriotism man-
ufactured on a man's own premises, Patriotism reasoned out in the man's own head and fire-assayed
and tested and proved in his own conscience. The
resulting Patriotism was a shop-worn product procured at second hand. The Patriot did not know
just how or when or where he got his opinions,
neither did he care, so long as he was with what
seemed the majority—which was the main thing,
the safe thing, the comfortable thing. Does the
reader believe he knows three men who have ac-
tual reasons for their pattern of Patriotism—and
can furnish them? Let him not examine, unless he

wants to be disappointed. He will be likely to find that his men got their Patriotism at the public trough, and had no hand in its preparation themselves.

Training does wonderful things. It moved the people of this country to oppose the Mexican War: then moved them to fall in with what they supposed was the opinion of the majority—majority Patriotism is the customary Patriotism—and go down there and fight. Before the Civil War it made the North indifferent to slavery and friendly to the slave interest; in that interest it made Massachusetts hostile to the American flag, and she would not allow it to be hoisted on her State House—in her eyes it was the flag of a faction. Then by and by training swung Massachusetts the other way, and she went raging South to fight under that very flag and against that aforetime-protected interest of hers.

There is nothing that training cannot do. Nothing is above its reach or below it. It can turn bad morals to good, good morals to bad; it can destroy principles, it can recreate them; it can debase angels to men and lift men to angelship. And it can do any one of these miracles in a year—even in six months.

Then men can be trained to manufacture their

own Patriotism. They can be trained to labor it out in their own heads and hearts and in the privacy and independence of their own premises. It can train them to stop taking it by command, as the Austrian takes his religion.

EUROPE AND ELSEWHERE (1900)

Vienna, January 9, 1899

Dear Mr. Stead,

Peace by compulsion. That seems a better idea than the other. Peace by persuasion has a pleasant sound, but I think we should not be able to work it. We should have to tame the human race first, and history seems to show that that cannot be done. Can't we reduce the armaments little by little—on a pro rata basis—by concert of the powers? Can't we get four great powers to agree to re-duce their strength 10 percent a year and thrash the others into doing likewise? For, of course, we cannot expect all of the powers to be in their right minds at one time. It has been tried. We are not going to try to get all of them to go into the scheme peaceably, are we? In that case I must withdraw my influence; because, for business reasons, I must preserve the outward signs of sanity. Four is enough if they can be securely harnessed together. They can compel peace, and peace without compulsion would be against nature and not operative. A sliding scale of reduction of 10 percent a year has a sort of plausible look, and I am willing to try that if three other powers will join. I feel sure that the armaments are now many times greater than necessary for the requirements of either peace or war. Take war-time for instance. Suppose circumstances made it necessary for us to fight another Waterloo, and that it would do what it did before— settle a large question and bring peace. I will guess that 400,000 men were on hand at Waterloo (I have forgotten the figures). In five hours they disabled 50,000 men. It took them that tedious, long time because the firearms delivered only two or three shots a minute. But we would do the work now as it was done at Omdurman, with shower guns, raining 600 balls a minute. Four men to a gun—is that the number? A hundred and fifty shots a minute per man. Thus a modern soldier is 149 Waterloo soldiers in one. Thus, also, we can now retain one man out of each 150 in service, disband the others, and fight our Waterloos just as effectively as we did eighty-five years ago. We should do the same beneficent job with 2,800 men now that we did with 400,000 then. The allies could take 1,400 of the men, and give Napoleon 1,400 and then whip him.

But instead what do we see? In war-time in Germany, Russia and France, taken together we find about 8 million men equipped for the field. Each man represents 149 Waterloo men, in usefulness and killing capacity. Altogether they constitute about 350 million Waterloo men, and there are not quite that many grown males of the human race now on this planet. Thus we have this insane fact—that whereas those three countries could arm 18,000 men with modern weapons and make them the equals of 3 million men of Napoleon's day, and accomplish with them all necessary war work, they waste their money and their prosperity creating forces of their populations in piling together 349,982,000 extra Waterloo equivalents which they would have no sort of use for if they would only stop drinking and sit down and cipher a little.

Perpetual peace we cannot have on any terms, I suppose; but I hope we can gradually reduce the war strength of Europe till we get it down to where it ought to be—20,000 men, properly armed. Then we can have all the peace that is worthwhile, and when we want a war anybody can afford it.

P.S. In the article I sent the figures are

wrong—"350 million" ought to be 450 million; "349,982,000" ought to be 449,982,000, and the remark about the sum being a little more than the present number of males on the planet—that is wrong, of course; it represents really one and a half the existing males.

Letter to William T. Stead,
MARK TWAIN'S LETTERS (1889)

3

Racism and Imperialism

Having now laid all the historical facts before the Person Sitting in Darkness, we should bring him to again, and explain them to him. We should say to him:

"They look doubtful, but in reality they are not. There have been lies; yes, but they were told in a good cause. We have been treacherous; but that was only in order that real good might come out of apparent evil. True, we have crushed a deceived and confiding people; we have turned against the weak and the friendless who trusted us; we have stamped out a just and intelligent and well-ordered republic; we have stabbed an ally in the back and slapped the face of a guest; we have bought a Shadow from an enemy that hadn't it to sell; we have robbed a trusting friend of his land and his liberty; we have invited our clean young men to shoulder a discredited musket and do bandits' work under a flag which bandits have been accustomed to fear, not to follow; we have debauched America's honor and blackened her face before the world; but each detail was for the best. We know this. The Head of every State and Sovereignty in Christendom and 90 percent of every legislative body in Christendom, including our Congress and our fifty State legislatures, are members not only of the church, but also of the Blessings-of-Civilization Trust. This world-girdling accumulation of trained morals, high principles, and justice cannot do an unright thing, an unfair thing, an ungenerous thing, an unclean thing. It knows what it is about. Give yourself no uneasiness; it is all right."

"To The Person Sitting in Darkness,"
NORTH AMERICAN REVIEW (1901)
(Reprinted in EUROPE AND ELSEWHERE)

There are many humorous things in the world; among them the white man's notion that he is less savage than the other savages.

FOLLOWING THE EQUATOR, Chapter XXI

The great bulk of the savages must go. The white man wants their lands, and all must go excepting such percentage of them as he will need to do his work for him upon terms to be determined by himself. Since history has removed the element of guesswork from this matter and made it certainty, the humanest way of diminishing the black population should be adopted, not the old cruel ways of the past. Mr. Rhodes and his gang have been following the old ways. They are chartered to rob and slay, and they lawfully do it, but not in a compassionate and Christian spirit. They rob the Mashonas and the Matabeles of a portion of their territories in the hallowed old style of "purchase" for a song, and then they force a quarrel and take the rest by the strong hand. They rob the natives of their cattle under the pretext that all the cattle in the country belonged to the king whom they have tricked and assassinated. They issue "regulations" requiring the incensed and harassed natives to work for the white settlers, and neglect their own affairs to do it. This is slavery, and is several times worse than was the American slavery which used to pain England so much; for when this Rhodesian slave is sick, superannuated, or otherwise disabled, he must support himself or starve—his master is under no obligation to support him.

The reduction of the population by Rhodesian methods to the desired limit is a return to the old-time slow-misery and lingering-death system of a discredited time and a crude "civilization." We humanely reduce an overplus of dogs by swift chloroform; the Boer humanely reduced an overplus of blacks by swift suffocation; the nameless but right-hearted Australian pioneer humanely reduced his overplus of aboriginal neighbors by a sweetened swift death concealed in a poisoned pudding. All these are admirable, and worthy of praise; you and I would rather suffer either of these deaths thirty times over in thirty successive days than linger out one of the Rhodesian twenty-year deaths, with its daily burden of insult, humiliation, and forced labor for a man whose entire race the victim hates. Rhodesia is a happy name for that land of piracy and pillage, and puts the right stain upon it.

FOLLOWING THE EQUATOR, Chapter LXVIII

All the territorial possessions of all the political establishments in the earth—including American, of course—consist of pilferings from other people's wash. No tribe, however insignificant, and no nation, howsoever mighty, occupies a foot of land that was not stolen. When the English, the French, and the Spaniards reached America, the Indian tribes had been raiding each other's territorial clothes-lines for ages, and every acre of ground in the continent had been stolen and restolen five hundred times. The English, the French, and the Spaniards went to work and stole it all over again; and when that was satisfactorily accomplished they went diligently to work and stole it from each other. In Europe and Asia and Africa every acre of ground has been stolen several millions of times. A crime persevered in a thousand centuries ceases to be a crime, and becomes a virtue. This is the law of custom, and custom supersedes all other forms of law.

FOLLOWING THE EQUATOR, Chapter LXIII

Africa has been as coolly divided up and portioned out among the gang as if they had bought it and paid for it. And now straightway they are beginning the old game again—to steal each other's grabbings. Germany found a vast slice of Central Africa with the English flag and the English missionary and the English trader scattered all over it, but with certain formalities neglected—no signs up, "Keep off the grass," "Trespassers forbidden," etc.—and she stepped in with a cold calm smile and put up the signs herself, and swept those English pioneers promptly out of the country.

There is a tremendous point there. It can be put into the form of a maxim: Get your formalities right—never mind about the moralities.

FOLLOWING THE EQUATOR, Chapter LXIII

4

Religion

Religion had its share in the changes of civilization and national character, of course. What share? The lion's. In the history of the human race this has always been the case, will always be the case, to the end of time, no doubt; or at least until man by the slow processes of evolution shall develop into something really fine and high—some billions of years hence, say.

"Bible Teaching and Religious Practice,"
EUROPE AND ELSEWHERE

The Christian's Bible is a drug store. Its contents remain the same; but the medical practice changes. For eighteen hundred years these changes were slight—scarcely noticeable. . . .

Not until far within our century was any considerable change in the practice introduced; and then mainly, or in effect only, in Great Britain and the United States. In the other countries to-day, the patient either still takes the ancient treatment or does not call the physician at all. In the English-speaking countries the changes observable in our century were forced by that very thing just referred to—the revolt of the patient against the system; they were not projected by the physician. The patient fell to doctoring himself, and the physician's practice began to fall off. He modified his method to get back his trade. He did it gradually, reluctantly; and never yielded more at a time than the pressure compelled. At first he relinquished the daily dose of hell and damnation, and administered it every other day only; next he allowed another day to pass; then another and presently another; when he had restricted it at last to Sundays, and imagined that now there would surely be a truce, the homeopath arrived on the field and made him abandon hell and damnation altogether, and administered Christ's love, and comfort, and charity and compassion in its stead. These had been in the drug store all the time, gold labeled and conspicuous among the long shelfloads of repulsive purges and vomits and poisons, and so the practice was to blame that they had remained unused, not the pharmacy. To the ecclesiastical physician of fifty years ago, his predecessor for eighteen centuries was a quack; to the ecclesiastical physician of to-day, his predecessor of fifty years ago was a quack. To the every-man-his-own-ecclesiastical-doctor of—when?—what will the ecclesiastical physician of to-day be? Unless evolution, which has been a truth ever since the globes, suns, and planets of the solar system were but wandering films of meteor dust, shall reach a limit and become a lie, there is but one fate in store for him.

The methods of the priest and the parson have been very curious, their history is very entertaining. In all the ages the Roman Church has owned slaves, bought and sold slaves, authorized and encouraged her children to trade in them. Long after some Christian peoples had freed their slaves the Church still held on to hers. If any could know, to absolute certainty, that all this was right, and according to God's will and desire, surely it was she, since she was God's specially appointed representative in the earth and sole authorized and infallible expounder of his Bible. There were the texts; there was no mistaking their meaning; she was right, she was doing in this thing what the Bible had mapped out for her to do. So unassailable was her position that in all the centuries she had no word to say against human slavery. Yet now at last, in our immediate day, we hear a Pope saying slave trading is wrong, and we see him sending an expedition to Africa to stop it. The texts remain: it is the practice that has changed. Why? Because the world has corrected the Bible. The Church never corrects it; and also never fails to drop in at the tail of the procession—and take the credit of the correction. As she will presently do in this instance.

Christian England supported slavery and encouraged it for two hundred and fifty years, and her Church's consecrated ministers looked on, sometimes taking an active hand, the rest of the time indifferent. England's interest in the business may be called a Christian interest, a Christian industry. She had her full share in its revival after a long period of inactivity, and this revival was a Christian monopoly; that is to say, it was in the hands of Christian countries exclusively. . . .

But at last in England, an illegitimate Christian rose against slavery. It is curious that when a Christian rises against a rooted wrong at all, he is usually an illegitimate Christian, member of some despised and bastard sect. There was a bitter struggle, but in the end the slave trade had to go—and went. The Biblical authorization remained, but the practice changed.

Then—the usual thing happened; the visiting English critic among us began straightway to hold up his pious hands in horror at our slavery. His distress was unappeasable, his words full of bitterness and contempt. It is true we had not so many as fifteen hundred thousand slaves for him to worry about, while his England still owned twelve millions, in her foreign possessions; but that fact did not modify his wail any, or stay his tears, or soften his censure. The fact that every time we had tried to get rid of our slavery in previous generations, but had always been obstructed, balked, and defeated by England, was a matter of no consequence to him; it was ancient history, and not worth the telling.

Our own conversion came at last. We began to stir against slavery. Hearts grew soft, here, there, and yonder. There was no place in the land where the seeker could not find some small budding sign of pity for the slave. No place in all the land but one—the pulpit. It yielded at last; it always does. It fought a strong and stubborn fight, and then did what it always does, joined the procession—at the tail end. Slavery fell. The slavery text remained; the practice changed, that was all.

During many ages there were witches. The Bible said so. The Bible commanded that they should not be allowed to live. Therefore the Church, after doing its duty in but a lazy and indolent way for eight hundred years, gathered up its halters, thumbscrews, and firebrands, and set about its holy work in earnest. She worked hard at it night and day during nine centuries and imprisoned, tortured, hanged, and burned whole hordes and armies of witches, and washed the Christian world clean with their foul blood.

Then it was discovered that there was no such thing as witches, and never had been. One does not know whether to laugh or to cry. Who discovered that there was no such thing as a witch—the priest, the parson? No, these never discover anything. At Salem, the parson clung pathetically to his witch text after the laity had abandoned it in remorse and tears for the crimes and cruelties it had persuaded them to do. The parson wanted more blood, more shame, more brutalities; it was the unconsecrated laity that stayed his hand. In Scotland the parson killed the witch after the magistrate had pronounced her innocent; and when the merciful legislature proposed to sweep the hideous laws against witches from the statute book, it was the parson who came imploring, with tears and imprecations, that they be suffered to stand.

There are no witches. The witch text remains; only the practice has changed. Hell fire is gone, but the text remains. Infant damnation is gone, but the text remains. More than two hundred death penalties are gone from the law books, but the texts that authorized them remain.

Is it not well worthy of note that of all the multitude of texts through which man has driven his annihilating pen he has never once made the mistake of obliterating a good and useful one? It does certainly seem to suggest that if man continues in the direction of enlightenment, his religous practice may, in the end, attain some semblance of human decency.

"Bible Teaching and Religious Practice,"
EUROPE AND ELSEWHERE

[In Germany] they recognize two sects, Catholic and Lutheran. . . . These receive State support; and their schools receive State support. Other sects are taxed to support these sects and schools, and have to run their own churches and schools at their own cost. It is infamous.

Just as infamous as it is with us—where no church property is taxed and so the infidel and the atheist and the man without religion are taxed to make up the deficit in the public income thus caused.

MARK TWAIN'S NOTEBOOK, Chapter XXI

The impromptu reason furnished by the early prophets of whom I have spoken was this:
"There is nothing *to* Christian Science; there

is nothing about it that appeals to the intellect; its market will be restricted to the unintelligent, the mentally inferior, the people who do not think."

They called that a reason why the cult would not flourish and endure. It seems the equivalent of saying:

"There is no money in tinware; there is nothing about it that appeals to the rich; its market will be restricted to the poor."

It is like bringing forward the best reason in the world why Christian Science should flourish and live, and then blandly offering it as a reason why it should sicken and die.

That reason was furnished me by the complacent and unfrightened prophets four years ago, and it has been furnished me again to-day. If conversions to new religions or to old ones were in any considerable degree achieved through the intellect, the aforesaid reason would be sound and sufficient, no doubt; the inquirer into Christian Science might go away unconvinced and unconverted. But we all know that conversions are seldom made in that way; that such a thing as a serious and painstaking and fairly competent inquiry into the claims of a religion or of a political dogma is a rare occurrence; and that the vast mass of men and women are far from being capable of making such an examination. They are not capable, for the reason that their minds, howsoever good they may be, are not trained for such examinations. The mind not trained for that work is no more competent to do it than are lawyers and farmers competent to make successful clothes without learning the tailor's trade. There are seventy-five million men and women among us who do not know how to cut out and make a dress-suit, and they would not think of trying; yet they all think they can competently think out a political or religious scheme without any apprenticeship to the business, and many of them believe they have actually worked that miracle. But, indeed, the truth is, almost all the men and women of our nation or of any other get their religion and their politics where they get their astronomy—entirely at second hand. Being untrained, they are no more able to intelligently examine a dogma or a policy than they are to calculate an eclipse.

Men are usually competent thinkers along the lines of their specialized training only. Within these limits alone are their opinions and judgments valuable; outside of these limits they grope and are lost—usually without knowing it.

CHRISTIAN SCIENCE, Book I, Chapter IX

My first American ancestor, Gentlemen, was an Indian—an early Indian. Your ancestors skinned him alive, and I am an orphan. Later ancestors of mine were the Quakers, William Robinson, Marmaduke Stevenson, *et. al.* Your tribe chased them out of the country for their religion's sake; promised them death if they came back; for your ancestors had forsaken the homes they loved, and braved the perils of the sea, the implacable climate, and the savage wilderness, to acquire that highest and most precious of boons, freedom for every man on this broad continent to worship according to the dictates of his own conscience—and they were not going to allow a lot of pestiferous Quakers to interfere with it. Your ancestors broke forever the chains of political slavery, and gave the vote to every man in this wide land, excluding none!—none except those who did not belong to the orthodox church. Your ancestors—yes, they were a hard lot; but nevertheless, they gave us religious liberty to worship as they required us to worship, and political liberty to vote as the church required; and so I the bereft one, I the forlorn one, am here to do my best to help you celebrate them right.

> Speech at the first annual dinner of the
> New England Society,
> MARK TWAIN'S SPEECHES
> (December 22, 1881)

We do not trust in God, in the important matters of life, and not even a minister of the Gospel will take any coin for a cent more than its accepted value because of that motto.

MARK TWAIN: A BIOGRAPHY,
Chapter CCLXVII

5

Conformity and Progress

The universal brotherhood of man is our most precious possession, what there is of it.

Pudd'nhead Wilson's New Calendar,
FOLLOWING THE EQUATOR, Chapter XXVII

Yes, oh yes, I am not overlooking the "steady progress from age to age of the coming of the kingdom of God and righteousness." "From age to age"— yes, it describes that giddy gait. I (and the rocks) will not live to see it arrive, but that is all right— it will arrive, it surely will. But you ought not to be always ironically apologizing for the Deity. If that thing is going to arrive, it is inferable that He wants it to arrive; and so it is not quite kind of you, and it hurts me, to see you flinging sarcasms at the gait of it. And yet it would not be fair in me not to admit that the sarcasms are deserved. When the Deity wants a thing, and after working at it for "ages and ages" can't show even a shade of progress toward its accomplishment, we—well, we don't laugh, but it is only because we dasn't. The source of "righteousness"—is in the heart? Yes. And engineered and directed by the brain? Yes. Well, history and tradition testify that the heart is just about what it was in the beginning; it has undergone no shade of change. Its good and evil impulses and their consequences are the same to-day that they were in the Old Bible times, in Egyptian times, in Greek times, in Middle Age times, in Twentieth Century times. There has been no change.

Meantime, the brain has undergone no change. It is what it always was. There are a few good brains and a multitude of poor ones. It was so in Old Bible times and in all other times—Greek, Roman, Middle Ages, and Twentieth Century. Among the savages—all the savages—the average brain is as competent as the average brain here or elsewhere. I will prove it to you, some time, if you like. And there are great brains among them, too. I will prove that also, if you like.

Well, the 19th century made progress—the first progress after "ages and ages"—colossal progress. In what? Materialities. Prodigious acquisitions were made in things which add to the comfort of many and make life harder for as many more. But the addition to righteousness? Is that discoverable? I think not. The materialities were not invented in the interest of righteousness; that there is more righteousness in the world because of them than there was before, is hardly demonstrable, I think. In Europe and America there is a cast change (due to them) in ideals—do you admire it? All Europe and all America are feverishly scrambling for money. Money is the supreme ideal—all others take tenth place with the great bulk of the nations named. Money-lust has always existed, but not in the history of the world was it ever a craze, a madness, until your time and mine. This lust has rotted these nations; it has made them hard, sordid, ungentle, dishonest, oppressive.

Did England rise against the infamy of the Boer war? No—rose in favor of it. Did America rise against the infamy of the Philippine war? No—rose in favor of it. Did Russia rise against the infamy of the present war? No—sat still and said nothing. Has the Kingdom of God advanced in Russia since the beginning of time?

Or in Europe and America, considering the vast backward step of the money-lust? Or anywhere else? If there has been any progress toward

righteousness since the early days of Creation—
which, in my ineradicable honesty, I am obliged to
doubt—I think we must confine it to ten percent of
the populations of Christendom (but leaving Russia, Spain, and South America entirely out). This
gives us 320,000,000 to draw the ten percent from.
That is to say, 32,000,000 have advanced toward
righteousness and the Kingdom of God since the
"ages and ages" have been flying along, the Deity
sitting up there admiring. Well, you see it leaves
1,200,000,000 out of the race. They stand just
where they have always stood, there has been no
change.

N.B. No charge for these informations. Do
come down soon, Joe.

Letter to Rev. J. H. Twitchell,
Hartford, Connecticut,
MARK TWAIN'S LETTERS (March 14, 1905)

How stunning are the changes which age makes in
man while he sleeps! When I finished Carlyle's
French Revolution in 1871 I was a Girondin; every
time I have read it since I have read it differently—
being influenced & changed, little by little, by life
& environment (& Taine & St. Simon); & now I
lay the book down once more, & recognize that I

am a Sansculotte!—And not a pale, characterless Sansculotte, but a Marat. Carlyle teaches no such gospel, so the change is in *me*—in my vision of the evidences.

Letter to William Dean Howells,
MARK TWAIN'S LETTERS (August 22, 1887)

Some men worship rank, some worship heroes, some worship power, some worship God, and over these ideals they dispute—but they all worship money.

MARK TWAIN'S NOTEBOOK, Chapter XXXI

Statement by Satan, the Devil's nephew:
"Oh, it's true. I know your race. It is made up of sheep. It is governed by minorities, seldom or never by majorities. It suppresses its feelings and its beliefs and follows the handful that makes the most noise. Sometimes the noisy handful is right, sometimes wrong; but no matter, the crowd follows it. The vast majority of the race, whether savage or civilized, are secretly kind-hearted and shrink from inflicting pain, but in the presence of the aggressive and pitiless minority they don't dare to assert themselves.

". . . you will always be and remain slaves of minorities."

THE MYSTERIOUS STRANGER, Chapter IX

I believe that . . . my notion of the Boer was rightly conceived. He is popularly called uncivilized, I do not know why. Happiness, food, shelter, clothing, wholesale labor, modest and rational ambitions, honesty, kindliness, hospitality, love of freedom and limitless courage to fight for it, composure and fortitude in time of disaster, patience in time of hardship and privation, absence of noise and brag in time of victory, contentment with a humble and peaceful life void of insane excitements—if there is a higher and better form of civilization than this, I am not aware of it and do not know where to look for it. I suppose we have the habit of imagining that a lot of artistic, intellectual, and other artificialities must be added, or it isn't complete. We and the English have these latter; but as we lack the great bulk of these others, I think the Boer civilization is the best of the two.

Letter to Rev. J. H. Twitchell

MARK TWAIN'S LETTERS (January 27, 1900)

There is no use in stringing out the details. The earl put us up and sold us at auction. This same infernal law had existed in our own South in my own time, more than thirteen hundred years later, and under it hundreds of freemen who could not prove that they were freemen had been sold into lifelong slavery without the circumstance making any particular impression upon me; but the minute law and the auction block came into my personal experience, a thing which had been merely improper before became suddenly hellish. Well, that's the way we are made.

A CONNECTICUT YANKEE IN KING ARTHUR'S
COURT, Chapter XXXIV

And so Missouri has fallen, that great state! Certain of her children have joined the lynchers, and the smirch is upon the rest of us. That handful of her children have given us a character and labeled us with a name, and to the dwellers in the four quarters of the earth we are "lynchers," now, and ever shall be. For the world will not stop and think—it never does, it is not its way; its way is to generalize from a single sample. It will not say, "Those Missourians have been busy eight years in building an honorable good name for themselves; these hundred lynchers down in the corner of the state are not real Missourians, they are renegades." No, that truth will not enter its mind; it will generalize from the one or two misleading samples and say, "The Missourians are lynchers." It has no reflection, no logic, no sense of proportion.

Why has lynching, with various barbaric accompaniments, become a favorite regulator in cases of "the usual crime" in several parts of the country? Is it because men think a lurid and terrible punishment a more forcible object lesson and a more effective deterrent than a sober and colorless hanging done privately in a jail would be? Surely sane men do not think that. Even the average child should know better. . . .

It must be that the increase [in lynching] comes of the inborn human instinct to imitate— that and man's commonest weakness, his aversion to being unpleasantly conspicuous, pointed at, shunned, as being on the unpopular side. Its other name is Moral Cowardice, and is the commanding feature of the make-up of 9,999 men in the 10,000. I am not offering this as a discovery; privately the dullest of us knows it to be true. History will not allow us to forget or ignore this supreme trait of our character. It persistently and sardonically reminds us that from the beginning of the world no revolt against a public infamy or oppression has ever been begun but by the one daring man in the 10,000, the rest timidly waiting, and slowly and reluctantly joining, under the influence of that man and his fellows from the other ten thousands. The abolitionists remember. Privately the public feeling was with them early, but each man was afraid to speak out until he got some hint that his neighbor was privately feeling as he privately felt himself. Then the boom followed. It always does. It will occur in New York, some day; and even in Pennsylvania.

It has been supposed—and said—that the people at a lynching enjoy the spectacle and are glad of a chance to see it. It cannot be true; all experience is against it. The people in the South are made like the people in the North—the vast majority of whom are right-hearted and compassionate, and would be cruelly pained by such a spectacle—and *would attend it*, and let on to be pleased with it, if the public approval seemed to require it. We are made like that, and we cannot help it. The other animals are not so, but we cannot help that, either. They lack the Moral Sense; we have no way of trading ours off, for a nickel or some other thing above its value. The Moral Sense teaches us what is right, and how to avoid it—when unpopular.

It is thought, as I have said, that a lynching crowd enjoys a lynching. It certainly is not true; it is impossible of belief. It is freely asserted—you have seen it in print many times of late—that the lynching impulse has been misinterpreted; that it is *not* the outcome of a spirit of revenge, but of a "mere atrocious hunger *to look upon* human suffering." If that were so, the crowds that saw the Windsor Hotel burn down would have enjoyed the horrors that fell under their eyes. Did they? No one will think that of them, no one will make that charge. Many risked their lives to save the men and women who were in peril. Why did they do that? Because *none would disapprove.* There was no restraint; they could follow their natural impulse. Why does a crowd of the same kind of people in Texas, Colorado, Indiana, stand by, smitten to the heart and miserable, and by ostentatious outward signs pretend to enjoy a lynching? Why does it lift no hand or voice in protest? Only because it would be unpopular to do it, I think; each man is afraid of his neighbor's disapproval—a thing which, to the general run of the race, is more dreaded than wounds and death. When there is to be a lynching the people hitch up and come miles to see it, bringing their wives and children. Really to see it? No—they come only because they are afraid to stay at home, lest it be noticed and offensively commented upon. We may believe this, for we all know how *we* feel about such spectacles— also, how we would act under the like pressure. We are not any better nor any braver than anybody else, and we must not try to creep out of it.

. . . [P]erhaps the remedy for lynchings comes to this: station a brave man in each affected community to encourage, support, and bring to light the deep disapproval of lynching hidden in the secret places of its heart—for it is there, beyond question. Then those communities will find something better to imitate—of course, being human, they must imitate something. Where shall these brave men be found? That is indeed a difficulty; there are not three hundred of them in the earth. If merely *physically* brave men would do, then it were easy; they could be furnished by the cargo. When Hobson called for seven volunteers to go with him to what promised to be certain death, four thousand men responded—the whole fleet, in fact. Because *all the world would approve.* They knew that; but if Hobson's project had been charged with the scoffs and jeers of the friends and associates, whose good opinion and approval the sailors valued, he could not have got his seven.

No, upon reflection, the scheme will not work. There are not enough morally brave men in stock. We are out of moral-courage material; we are in a condition of profound poverty. We have those two sheriffs down South who—but never mind, it is not enough to go around; they have to stay and take care of their own communities.

But if we only *could* have three or four more sheriffs of that great breed! Would it help? I think so. For we are all imitators: other brave sheriffs would follow; to be a dauntless sheriff would come to be recognized as the correct and only thing, and the dreaded disapproval would fall to the share of the other kind; courage in this office would become custom, the absence of it a dishonor, just as courage presently replaces the timidity of the new soldier; then the mobs and the lynchings would disappear, and—

However. It can never be done without some starters, and where are we to get the starters? Advertise? Very well, then, let us advertise.

"The United States of Lyncherdom,"
EUROPE AND ELSEWHERE (1901)

Man has not a single right which is the product of anything but might.

Not a single right is indestructible: a new might can at any time abolish it, hence, man possesses not a single *permanent* right.

MARK TWAIN'S NOTEBOOK, Chapter XXXV

Two or three weeks ago Elinor Glyn called on me one afternoon and we had a long talk, of a distinctly unusual character, in the library. . . .

I talked to her with daring frankness, frequently calling a spade a spade instead of coldly symbolizing it as a snow shovel. . . . I . . . said I couldn't call to mind a written law of any kind that had been promulgated in any age of the world in any statute book or any Bible for the regulation of man's conduct in *any* particular, from assassination all the way up to Sabbath-breaking, that wasn't a violation of the law of Nature, which I regarded as the highest of laws, the most peremptory and absolute of all laws—Nature's laws being in my belief plainly and simply the laws of God, since He instituted them, He and no other, and the said laws, by authority of this divine origin taking precedence of all the statutes of man.

. . . I said we were the servants of convention; that we could not subsist, whether in a savage or a civilized state, without conventions; that we must accept them and stand by them, even when we disapproved of them; that while the laws of Nature, that is to say the laws of God, plainly made every human being a law unto himself, we must steadfastly refuse to obey those laws, and we must as steadfastly stand by the conventions which ignore them, since the statutes furnish us peace, fairly good government, and stability, and therefore are better for us than the laws of God, which would soon plunge us into confusion and disorder and anarchy, if we should adopt them. I said her book was an assault upon certain old and well-established and wise conventions, and that it would not find many friends, and indeed would not deserve many.

She said I was brave, the bravest person she had ever met (gross flattery which could have beguiled me when I was very very young), and she implored me to publish these views of mine, but I said, "No, such a thing is unthinkable." I said that if I, or any other wise, intelligent, and experienced person, should suddenly throw down the walls that protect and conceal his *real* opinions on almost any subject under the sun, it would at once be perceived that he had lost his intelligence and his wisdom and ought to be sent to the asylum. I said I had been revealing to her my private sentiments, *not* my public ones; that I, like all the other human beings, expose to the world only my trimmed and perfumed and carefully barbered public opinions and conceal carefully, cautiously, wisely, my private ones.

I explained that what I meant by that phrase "public opinions" was *published* opinions, opinions spread broadcast in print. I said I was in the common habit, in private conversation with friends, of revealing every private opinion I possessed relating to religion, politics, and men, but that I should never dream of *printing* one of them, because they are individually and collectively at war with almost everybody's public opinion, while at the same time they are in happy agreement with almost everybody's private opinion. As an instance, I asked her if she had ever encountered an intelligent person who privately believed in the Immaculate Conception—which of course she hadn't; and I also asked her if she had ever seen an intelligent person who was daring enough to publicly deny his belief in that fable and print the denial. Of course she hadn't encountered any such person.

I said I had a large cargo of most interesting and important private opinions about every great matter under the sun, but that they were not for print. I reminded her that we all break over the rule two or three times in our lives and fire a disagreeable and unpopular private opinion of ours into print, but we never do it when we can help it, we never do it except when the desire to do it is too strong for us and overrides and conquers our cold, calm, wise judgment. She mentioned several instances in which I had come out publicly in defense of unpopular causes, and she intimated that what I had been saying about myself was not perhaps in strict accordance with the facts; but I said they were merely illustrations of what I had just been saying, that when I publicly attacked the American missionaries in China and some other iniquitous persons and causes, I did not do it for any reason but for just the one: that the inclination to do it was stronger than my diplomatic instincts, and I had to obey and take the consequences. But I said I was not moved to defend her book in public. . . .

The lady was young enough, and inexperienced enough, to imagine that whenever a person has an unpleasant opinion in stock which could be of educational benefit to Tom, Dick, and Harry, it is his *duty* to come out in print with it and become its champion. I was not able to convince her that we never do *any* duty for duty's sake but only for the mere personal satisfaction we get out of doing that duty. The fact is, she was brought up just like the rest of the world, with the ingrained and stupid superstition that there is such a thing as *duty for duty's sake*, and so I was obliged to let her abide in her darkness. She believed that when a man held a private unpleasant opinion of an educational sort, which would get him hanged if he published it, he ought to publish it anyway and was a coward if he didn't. Take it all around, it was a very pleasant conversation, and glaringly unprintable.

"Elinor Glyn," MARK TWAIN IN ERUPTION
(January 13, 1908)

Dr. Loeb's Incredible Discovery

Experts in biology will be apt to receive with some skepticism the announcement of Dr. Jacques Loeb of the University of California as to the creation of life by chemical agencies. . . . Doctor Loeb is a very bright and ingenious experimenter, but *a consensus of opinion among biologists* would show that he is voted rather as a man of lively imagination than an inerrant investigator of natural phenomena.

New York Times (March 2)

I wish I could be as young as that again. Although I seem so old now, I was once as young as that. I remember, as if it were but thirty or forty years ago, how a paralyzing Consensus of Opinion accumulated from Experts a-setting around, about brother experts who had patiently and laboriously cold-chiseled their way into one or another of nature's safe-deposit vaults and were reporting that they had found something valuable was a-plenty for me. It settled it.

But it isn't so now—no. Because, in the drift of the years I by and by found out that a Consensus examines a new thing with its feelings rather oftener than with its mind. You know, yourself, that

that is so. Do those people examine with feelings that are friendly to evidence? You know they don't. It is the other way about. They do the examining by the light of their prejudices—now isn't that true?

With curious results, yes. So curious that you wonder the Consensuses do not go out of the business. Do you know of a case where a Consensus won a game? You can go back as far as you want to and you will find history furnishing you this (until now) unwritten maxim for your guidance and profit: Whatever new thing a Consensus coppers [colloquial for "bets against"], bet your money on that very card and do not be afraid. . . .

This is warm work! It puts my temperature up to 106 and raises my pulse to the limit. It always works just so when the red rag of a Consensus jumps my fence and starts across my pasture. I have been a Consensus more than once myself, and I know the business—and its vicissitudes. I am a compositor-expert, of old and seasoned experience; nineteen years ago I delivered the final-and-for-good verdict that the linotype would never be able to earn its own living nor anyone else's: it takes fourteen acres of ground, now, to accommodate its factories in England. Thirty-five years ago I was an expert precious-metal quartz-miner.

There was an outcrop in my neighborhood that assayed $600 a ton—gold. But every fleck of gold in it was shut up tight and fast in an intractable and impersuadable base-metal shell. Acting as a Consensus, I delivered the finality verdict that no human ingenuity would ever be able to set free two dollars' worth of gold out of a ton of that rock. The fact is, I did not foresee the cyanide process. Indeed, I have been a Consensus ever so many times since I reached maturity and approached the age of discretion, but I call to mind no instance in which I won out.

These sorrows have made me suspicious of Consensuses. Do you know, I tremble and the goose flesh rises on my skin every time I encounter one, now. I sheer warily off and get behind something, saying to myself, "It looks innocent and all right, but no matter, ten to one there's a cyanide process under that thing somewhere."

Now as concerns this "creation of life by chemical agencies." Reader, take my advice: don't you copper it. I don't say bet on it; no, I only say, don't you copper it. As you see, there is a Consensus out against it. If you find that you can't control your passions; if you feel that you have *got* to copper something and can't help it, copper the Consensus. It is the safest way—all history confirms it. If you are young, you will, of course, have to put up, on the one side or the other, for you will not be able to restrain yourself; but as for me, I am old, and I am going to wait for a new deal.

EUROPE AND ELSEWHERE

Corn-Pone Opinions

Fifty years ago, when I was a boy of fifteen and helping to inhabit a Missourian village on the banks of the Mississippi, I had a friend whose society was very dear to me because I was forbidden by my mother to partake of it. He was a gay and impudent and satirical and delightful young black man—a slave—who daily preached sermons from the top of his master's woodpile, with me for sole audience. He imitated the pulpit style of the several clergymen of the village, and did it well, and with fine passion and energy. To me he was a wonder. I believed he was the greatest orator in the United States and would some day be heard from. But this did not happen; in the distribution of rewards he was overlooked. It is the way, in this world.

He interrupted his preaching, now and then, to saw a stick of wood; but the sawing was a pretense—he did it with his mouth; exactly imitating the sound the bucksaw makes in shrieking its way through the wood. But it served its purpose; it kept his master from coming out to see how the work was getting along. I listened to the sermons from the open window of a lumber room at the back of the house. One of his texts was this:

"You tell me whar a man gits his corn-pone, en I'll tell you what his 'pinions is."

I can never forget it. It was deeply impressed upon me. By my mother. Not upon my memory, but elsewhere. She had slipped in upon me while I was absorbed and not watching. The black philosopher's idea was that a man is not independent, and cannot afford views which might interfere with his bread and butter. If he would prosper, he must train with the majority; in matters of large moment, like politics and religion, he must think and feel with the bulk of his neighbors, or suffer damage in his social standing and in his business prosperities. He must restrict himself to corn-pone opinions—at least on the surface. He must get his opinions from other people; he must reason out none for himself; he must have no first-hand views.

I think Jerry was right, in the main, but I think he did not go far enough.

1. It was his idea that a man conforms to the majority view of his locality by calculation and intention.

This happens, but I think it is not the rule.

2. It was his idea that there is such a thing as a first-hand opinion; an original opinion; an opinion which is coldly reasoned out in man's head, by a searching analysis of the facts involved, with the heart unconsulted, and the jury room closed against outside influences. It may be that such an opinion has been born somewhere, at some time or other, but I suppose it got away before they could catch it and stuff it and put it in the museum.

I am persuaded that a coldly-thought-out and independent verdict upon a fashion in clothes, or manners, or literature, or politics, or religion, or any other matter that is projected into the field of our notice and interest, is a most rare thing—if it has indeed ever existed.

. . . The outside influences are always pouring in upon us, and we are always obeying their orders and accepting their verdicts. The Smiths like the new play; the Joneses go to see it, and they copy the Smith verdict. Morals, religions, politics, get their following from surrounding influences and atmospheres, almost entirely; not from study, not from thinking. A man must and will have his own approval first of all, in each and every moment and circumstance of his life—even if he must repent of a self-approved act the moment after its commission, in order to get his self-approval *again:* but, speaking in general terms, a man's self-approval in the large concerns of life has its source in the approval of the peoples about him, and not in a searching personal examination of the matter. Mohammedans are Mohammedans because they are born and reared among that sect, not because they have thought it out and can furnish sound reasons for being Mohammedans; we know why Catholics are Catholics; why Presbyterians are Presbyterians; why Baptists are Baptists; why Mormons are Mormons; why thieves are thieves; why monarchists are monarchists; why Republicans are Republicans and Democrats, Democrats. We know it is a matter of association and sympathy, not reasoning and examination; that hardly a man in the world has an opinion upon morals, politics, or religion which he got otherwise than through his associations and sympathies. Broadly speaking, there are none but corn-pone opinions. And broadly speaking, corn-pone stands for self-approval. Self-approval is acquired mainly from the approval of other people. The result is conformity. Sometimes conformity has a sordid business interest—the bread-and-butter interest—but not in most cases, I think. I think that in the majority of cases it is unconscious and not calculated; that it is born of the human being's natural yearning to stand well with his fellows and have their inspiring approval and praise—a yearning which is commonly so strong and so insistent that it cannot be effectually resisted, and must have its way.

A political emergency brings out the corn-pone opinion in fine force in its two chief varieties—the pocketbook variety, which has its origin in self-interest, and the bigger variety, the sentimental variety—the one which can't bear to be outside the pale; can't bear to be in disfavor; can't endure the averted face and the cold shoulder; wants to stand well with his friends, wants to be smiled upon, wants to be welcome, wants to hear the precious words, *"He's* on the right track!" Uttered, perhaps by an ass, but still an ass of high degree, an ass whose approval is gold and diamonds to a smaller ass, and confers glory and honor and happiness, and membership in the herd. For these gauds many a man will dump his life-long principles into the street, and his conscience along with them. We have seen it happen. In some millions of instances.

Men think they think upon great political questions, and they do; but they think with their party, not independently; they read its literature, but not that of the other side; they arrive at convictions, but they are drawn from a partial view of the matter in hand and are of no particular value. They swarm with their party, they feel with their party, they are happy in their party's approval, and where the party leads they will follow, whether for right and honor, or through blood and dirt and a mush of mutilated morals.

In our late canvass half of the nation passionately believed that in silver lay salvation, the other half as passionately believed that in that way lay destruction. Do you believe that a tenth part of the people, on either side, had any rational excuse for having an opinion about the matter at all? I studied that mighty question to the bottom—came out empty. Half of our people passionately believe in high tariff, the other half believe otherwise. Does this mean study and examination, or only feeling? The latter, I think. I have deeply studied that question, too—and didn't arrive. We all do no end of feeling, and we mistake it for thinking. And out of it we get an aggregation which we consider a boon. Its name is Public Opinion. It is held in reverence. It settles everything. Some think it the Voice of God.

EUROPE AND ELSEWHERE (1900)

Human nature being what it is, I suppose we must expect to drift into monarchy by and by. It is a saddening thought but we cannot change our nature—we are all alike, we human beings; and in our blood and bone, and ineradicably, we carry the seeds out of which monarchies and aristocracies are grown: worship of gauds, titles, distinctions, power. We have to worship these things and their possessors, we are all born so and we cannot help it. We have to be despised by somebody whom we regard as above us or we are not happy; we have to have somebody to worship and envy or we cannot be content. In America we manifest this in all the ancient and customary ways. In public we scoff at titles and hereditary privilege but privately we hanker after them, and when we get a chance we buy them for cash and a daughter.

. . . Like all the other nations we worship money and the possessors of it—they being our aristocracy, and we have to have one. We like to read about rich people in the papers; the papers know it, and they do their best to keep this appetite liberally fed. They even leave out a football game or a bull fight now and then to get room for all the particulars of how—according to the display heading—"Rich Woman Fell Down Cellar—Not Hurt." The falling down the cellar is of no interest to us when the woman is not rich but no rich woman can fall down a cellar and we not yearn to know all about it and wish it was us.

In a monarchy the people willingly and rejoicingly revere and take pride in their nobilities, and are not humiliated by the reflection that this humble and hearty homage gets no return but contempt. Contempt does not shame them, they are used to it and they recognize that it is their proper due. We are all made like that. In Europe we easily and quickly learn to take that attitude toward the sovereigns and the aristocracies; moreover, it has been observed that when we get the attitude we go on and exaggerate it, presently becoming more servile than the natives and vainer of it. The next step is to rail and scoff at republics and democracies. All of which is natural, for we have not ceased to be human beings by becoming Americans, and the human race was always intended to be governed by kingship, not by popular vote.

I suppose we must expect that unavoidable and irresistible Circumstances will gradually take away the powers of the States and concentrate them in the central government, and that the republic will then repeat the history of all time and become a monarchy; but I believe that if we obstruct these encroachments and steadily resist them the monarchy can be postponed for a while yet.

"The Drift Toward Centralized Power,"
MARK TWAIN IN ERUPTION
(December 13, 1906)

The human race was always interesting, and we know by its past that it will always continue so. Monotonously. It is always the same; it never changes. Its circumstances change from time to time, for better or worse, but the race's *character* is permanent, and never changes. In the course of the ages it has built up several great and worshipful civilizations and has seen unlooked-for circumstances slily emerge bearing deadly gifts which looked like benefits and were welcomed, whereupon the decay and destruction of each of these stately civilizations has followed.

It is not worthwhile to try to keep history from repeating itself, for man's character will always make the preventing of the repetitions impossible. Whenever man makes a large stride in material prosperity and progress he is sure to think that *he* has progressed, whereas he has not advanced an inch; nothing has progressed but his circumstances. *He* stands where he stood before. He knows more than his forebears knew but his intellect is no better than theirs and never will be. He is richer than his forebears but his character is no improvement upon theirs. Riches and education are not a permanent possession; they will pass away, as in the case of Rome and Greece and Egypt and Babylon; and a moral and mental midnight will follow—with a dull long sleep and a slow reawakening. From time to time he makes what looks like a change in his character but it is not a real change; and it is only transitory anyway. He cannot even invent a religion and keep it intact; circumstances are stronger than he and all his works. Circumstances and conditions are always changing, and they always compel him to modify his religions to harmonize with the new situation.

For twenty-five or thirty years I have squandered a deal of my time—too much of it perhaps—in trying to guess what is going to be the process which will turn our republic into a monarchy and how far off that even might be. Every man is a master and also a servant, a vassal. There is always someone who looks up to him and admires and envies him; there is always someone to whom he looks up and whom he admires and envies. This is his nature; this is his character; and it is unchangeable, indestructible; therefore republics and democracies are not for such as he; they cannot satisfy the requirements of his nature. The inspirations of his character will always breed circumstances and conditions which must in time furnish him a king and an aristocracy to look up to and worship. In a democracy he will try—and honestly—to keep the crown away, but Circumstance is a powerful master and will eventually defeat him.

Republics have lived long but monarchy lives forever. By our teaching we learn that vast material prosperity always brings in its train conditions which debase the morals and enervate the manhood of a nation—then the country's liberties come into the market and are bought, sold, squandered, thrown away, and a popular idol is carried to the throne upon the shields or shoulders of the worshiping people and planted there in permanency. We are always being taught—no, formerly we were always being taught—to look at Rome and beware. The teacher pointed to Rome's stern virtue, incorruptibility, love of liberty, and all-sacrificing patriotism—this when she was young and poor; then he pointed to her later days when her sunbursts of material prosperity and spreading dominion came and were exultingly welcomed by the people, they not suspecting that these were not fortunate glories, happy benefits, but were a disease and freighted with death.

The teacher reminded us that Rome's liberties were not auctioned off in a day, but were bought slowly, gradually, furtively, little by little; first with a little corn and oil for the exceedingly poor and wretched, later with corn and oil for voters who were not quite so poor, later still with corn and oil for pretty much every man that had a vote to sell—exactly our own history over again. At first we granted deserved pensions, righteously and with a clean and honorable motive, to the disabled soldiers of the Civil War. The clean motive began and ended there. We have made many and amazing additions to the pensions list but with a motive which dishonors the uniform and the Congresses which have voted the additions—the sole purpose back of the additions being the purchase of votes. It is corn and oil over again, and promises to do its full share in the eventual subversion of the republic and the substitution of monarchy in its place. The monarchy would come anyhow, without this, but this has a peculiar interest for us in that it prodigiously hastens the day. We have the two Roman conditions: stupendous wealth with its inevitable corruptions and moral blight, and the corn and oil pensions—that is to say, vote bribes, which have taken away the pride of thousands of tempted men and turned them into willing alms receivers and unashamed.

> "Purchasing Civic Virtue,"
> MARK TWAIN IN ERUPTION
> (January 15, 1907)

We are always hearing of people who are around *seeking* after Truth. I have never seen a (permanent) specimen. I think he has never lived. But I have seen several entirely sincere people who *thought* they were (permanent) Seekers after Truth. They sought diligently, persistently, carefully, cautiously, profoundly, with perfect honesty and nicely adjusted judgment—until they believed that without doubt or question they had found the Truth. *That was the end of the search.* The man spent the rest of his life hunting up shingles wherewith to protect his Truth from the weather. If he was seeking after political Truth he found it in one or another of the hundred political gospels which govern men in the earth; if he was seeking after the Only True Religion he found it in one or another of the three thousand that are on the market. In any case, when he found the Truth *he sought no further;* but from that day forth, with his soldering-iron in one hand and his bludgeon in the other he tinkered its leaks and reasoned with objectors. There have been innumerable Temporary Seekers after Truth—have you ever heard of a permanent one? In the very nature of man such a person is impossible. However, to drop back to the text—training: all training is one form or another of *outside* influence, and *association* is the largest part of it. A man is never anything but what his outside influences have made him. They train him downward or they train him upward—but they *train* him; they are at work upon him all the time.

WHAT IS MAN?, Chapter IV

6

Morality and Truth

March 14, '05

Dear Joe,

I have a Pudd'nhead maxim:

"When a man is a pessimist before 48 he knows too much; if he is an optimist after it, he knows too little."

It is with contentment, therefore, that I reflect that I am better and wiser than you. Joe, you seem to be dealing in "bulks," now; the "bulk" of the farmers and U.S. Senators are "honest." As regards purchase and sale with *money?* Who doubts it? Is that the only measure of honesty? Aren't there a dozen kinds of honesty which can't be measured by the money-standard? Treason is treason—and there's more than one form of it; the money-form is but one of them. When a person is disloyal to any confessed duty, he is plainly and simply dishonest, and knows it; knows it, and is privately troubled about it and not proud of himself. Judged by this standard—and who will challenge the validity of it?—there isn't an honest man in Connecticut, nor in the Senate, nor anywhere else. I do not even except myself, this time.

Am I finding fault with you and the rest of the populace? *No*—I assure you I am not. For I know the human race's limitations, and this makes it my duty—my pleasant duty—to be fair to it. Each person in it is honest in one or several ways, but no member of it is honest in all the ways required by—by what? *By his own standard.* Outside of that, as I look at it, there is no obligation upon him.

Am I honest? I give you my word of honor (private) I am not. For seven years I have suppressed a book which my conscience tells me I ought to publish. I hold it a duty to publish it. There are other difficult duties which I am equal to, but I am not equal to that one. Yes, even I am dishonest. Not in many ways, but in some. Forty-one, I think it is. We are certainly *all* honest in one or several ways—every man in the world—though I have reason to think I am the only one whose black-list runs so light. Sometimes I feel lonely enough in this lofty solitude.

Letter to Rev. J. H. Twitchell,
MARK TWAIN'S LETTERS (March 14, 1905)

For good or for evil we continue to educate Europe. We have held the post of instructor for more than a century and a quarter now. We were not elected to it, we merely took it. We are of the Anglo-Saxon race. At the banquet last winter of that organization which calls itself the Ends of the Earth Club, the chairman, a retired regular army officer of high grade, proclaimed in a loud voice, and with fervency, "We are of the Anglo-Saxon race, and when the Anglo-Saxon wants a thing *he just takes it.*"

That utterance was applauded to the echo. There were perhaps seventy-five civilians present and twenty-five military and naval men. It took those people nearly two minutes to work off their stormy admiration for that great sentiment; and meanwhile the inspired prophet who had discharged it—from his liver, or his intestines, or his esophagus, or wherever he had bred it—stood there glowing and beaming and smiling and issuing rays of happiness from every pore, rays that were so intense that they were visible and made him look like the old-time picture in the Almanac of the man who stands discharging signs of the zodiac in every direction, and so absorbed in happiness, so steeped in happiness, that he smiles and smiles and has plainly forgotten that he is painfully and dangerously ruptured and exposed amidships and needs sewing up right away.

The soldier man's great utterance, interpreted by the expression which he put into it, meant in plain English, "The English and the Americans are thieves, highwaymen, pirates, and we are proud to be of the combination."

Out of all the English and Americans present, there was not one with the grace to get up and say he was ashamed of being an Anglo-Saxon, and also ashamed of being a member of the human race since the race must abide under the presence upon it of the Anglo-Saxon taint. I could not perform this office. I could not afford to lose my temper and make a self-righteous exhibition of myself and my superior morals that I might teach this infant class in decency the rudiments of that cult, for they would not be able to grasp it; they would not be able to understand it. . . .

The initial welcome of that strange sentiment was not an unwary betrayal, to be repented of upon reflection; and this was shown by the fact that whenever during the rest of the evening a speaker found that he was becoming uninteresting and wearisome, he only needed to inject that great Anglo-Saxon moral into the midst of his platitudes to start up that glad storm again. After all, it was only the human race on exhibition. It has always been a peculiarity of the human race that it keeps two sets of morals in stock—the private and real, and the public and artificial.

Our public motto is "In God we trust," and when we see those gracious words on the trade-dollar (worth sixty cents) they always seem to tremble and whimper with pious emotion. That is our public motto. It transpires that our private one is, "When the Anglo-Saxon wants a thing *he just takes it.*" Our public morals are touchingly set forth in that stately and yet gentle and kindly motto which indicates that we are a nation of gracious and affectionate multitudinous brothers compacted into one—"*e pluribus unum.*" Our private morals find the light in the sacred phrase, "Come, *step* lively!"

. . . Something more than a century ago we gave Europe the first notions of liberty it had ever had, and thereby largely and happily helped to bring on the French Revolution and claim a share in its beneficent results. We have taught Europe many lessons since. But for us, Europe might never have known the interviewer; but for us certain of the European states might never have experienced the blessing of extravagant imposts; but for us the European Food Trust might never have acquired the art of poisoning the world for cash; but for us her Insurance Trusts might never have

found out the best way to work the widow and orphan for profit; but for us the long delayed re-
sumptions of Yellow Journalism in Europe might
have been postponed for generations to come.
Steadily, continuously, persistently, we are Amer-
icanizing Europe, and all in good time we shall get
the job perfected.

MARK TWAIN IN ERUPTION
(September 7,1906)

Shall we? That is, shall we go on conferring our
Civilization upon the peoples that sit in darkness,
or shall we give those poor things a rest? Shall we
bang right ahead in our old-time, loud, pious way,
and commit the new century to the game; or shall
we sober up and sit down and think it over first?
Would it not be prudent to get our Civilization
tools together, and see how much stock is left on
hand in the way of Glass Beads and Theology, and
Maxim Guns and Hymn Books, and Trade Gin and
Torches of Progress and Enlightenment (patent ad-
justable ones, good to fire villages with, upon oc-
casion), and balance the books, and arrive at the
profit and loss, so that we may intelligently decide
whether to continue the business or sell out the

property and start a new Civilization Scheme on the proceeds?

NORTH AMERICAN REVIEW, 1901
(Reprinted in EUROPE AND ELSEWHERE)

Day before yesterday's New York *Sun* has a paragraph or two from its London correspondent which enables me to locate myself. The correspondent mentions a few of our American events of the past twelvemonth, such as the limitless rottenness of our great insurance companies, where theft has been carried on by our most distinguished commercial men as a profession; the exposures of conscienceless graft, colossal graft, in great municipalities like Philadelphia, St. Louis, and other large cities; the recent exposure of millionfold graft in the great Pennsylvania Railway system—with minor uncoverings of commerical swindles from one end of the United States to the other; and finally today's lurid exposure, by Upton Sinclair, of the most titanic and death-dealing swindle of them all, the Beef Trust, an exposure which has moved the President to demand of a reluctant Congress a law which shall protect America and Europe from falling, in a mass, into the hands of the doctor and the undertaker.

According to that correspondent, Europe is beginning to wonder if there is really an honest male human creature left in the United States. A year ago I was satisfied that there was no such person existing upon American soil except myself. That exception has since been rubbed out, and now it is my belief that there isn't a single male human being in America who is honest. I held the belt all along, until last January. Then I went down, with Rockefeller and Carnegie and a group of Goulds and Vanderbilts and other professional grafters, and swore off my taxes like the most conscience-less of the lot. I was a great loss to America, because I was irreplaceable. It is my belief that it will take fifty years to produce my successor. I believe the entire population of the United States—exclusive of the women—to be rotten, as far as the dollar is concerned. Understand, I am saying these things as a dead person. I should consider it indiscreet in any live one to make these remarks publicly.

"Bret Harte," EUROPE AND ELSEWHERE
(June 13, 1906)

We have a criminal jury system which is superior to any in the world; and its efficiency is only marred by the difficulty of finding twelve men every day who don't know anything and can't read.

MARK TWAIN'S SPEECHES (July 4, 1872)

What is the difference between a taxidermist and a tax collector? The taxidermist takes only your skin.

MARK TWAIN'S NOTEBOOK, Chapter XXXIII

There is one thing that always puzzles me: as inheritors of the mentality of our reptile ancestors we have improved the inheritance by a thousand grades; but in the matter of the morals which they left us we have gone backward as many grades. That evolution is strange, and to me unaccountable and unnatural. Necessarily we started equipped with their perfect and blemishless morals; now we are wholly destitute; we have no real morals, but only artificial ones—morals created and preserved by the forced suppression of natural and hellish instincts. Yet we are dull enough to be vain of them. Certainly we are a sufficiently comical invention, we humans.

Letter to J. Howard Moore,
MARK TWAIN'S LETTERS (February 2, 1907)

The low level which commercial morality has reached in America is deplorable. We have humble God-fearing Christian men among us who will stoop to do things for a million dollars that they ought not to be willing to do for less than 2 millions.

MORE MAXIMS OF MARK

Jay Gould was the mightiest disaster which has ever befallen this country. The people had *desired* money before his day, but *he* taught them to fall down and worship it. They had respected men of means before his day, but along with this respect was joined the respect due to the character and industry which had accumulated it. But Jay Gould taught the entire nation to make a god of the money and the man, no matter how the money might have been acquired. In my youth there was nothing resembling a worship of money or of its possessor, in our region. And in our region no well-to-do man was ever charged with having acquired his money by shady methods.

The gospel left behind by Jay Gould is doing giant work in our days. Its message is "Get money.

Get it quickly. Get it in abundance. Get it in prodigious abundance. Get it dishonestly if you can,
honestly if you must."

> "The Teaching of Jay Gould,"
> MARK TWAIN IN ERUPTION
> (February 16, 1906)

The political and commercial morals of the United
States are not merely food for laughter, they are an
entire banquet. The human being is a curious and
interesting invention. It takes a Cromwell and
some thousands of preaching and praying soldiers
and parsons ten years to raise the standards of English official and commercial morals to a respect-
worthy altitude, but it takes only one Charles II a
couple of years to pull them down into the mud
again. Our standards were fairly high a generation
ago, and they had been brought to that grade by
some generations of wholesome labor on the part
of the nation's multitudinous teachers; but Jay
Gould, all by himself, was able to undermine the
structure in half a dozen years; and in thirty years
his little band of successors . . . have been able to

sodden it with decay from the roof to the cellar and render it shaky and beyond repair, apparently.

"The Teaching Applied,"
MARK TWAIN IN ERUPTION
(January 30, 1907)

Maxims in the Rough

None but the dead have free speech.
None but the dead are permitted to speak the truth.
In America—as elsewhere—free speech is confined to the dead.

MARK TWAIN'S NOTEBOOK, Chapter XXXV

All schools, all colleges, have two great functions: to confer, and to conceal valuable knowledge. The Theological knowledge which they conceal cannot justly be regarded as less valuable than that which they reveal. That is, if, when man is buying a basket of strawberries, it can profit him to know that the bottom half of it is rotten.

MARK TWAIN'S NOTEBOOK,
last entry (November 5, 1908)

It is strange and fine—Nature's lavish generosities to her creatures. At least to all of them except man. For those that fly she has provided a home that is nobly spacious—a home which is forty miles deep and envelops the whole globe, and has not an obstruction in it. For those that swim she has provided a more than imperial domain—a domain which is miles deep and covers four-fifths of the globe. But as for man, she has cut him off with the mere odds and ends of the creation. She has given him the thin skin, the meager skin which is stretched over the remaining one-fifth—the naked bones stick up through it in most places. On the one-half of this domain he can raise snow, ice, sand, rocks, and nothing else. So the valuable part of his inheritance really consists of but a single fifth of the family estate; and out of it he has to grub hard to get enough to keep him alive and provide kings and soldiers and powder to extend the blessings of civilization with. Yet man, in his simplicity and complacency and inability to cipher, thinks Nature regards him as the important member of the family—in fact, her favorite. Surely, it must occur to even his dull head, sometimes, that she has a curious way of showing it.

FOLLOWING THE EQUATOR, Chapter LXII

About the Author

Samuel Langhorne Clemens was born in Florida, Missouri on November 30, 1835. He spent his childhood in the Mississippi River town of Hannibal—a setting immortalized by Mark Twain in *Tom Sawyer.* Upon his father's death, he left school at age 12, working first as a printer's apprentice, and later, helping his elder brother run the local newspaper.

An itinerant wanderer and adventurer, Clemens spent his early years jumping from one occupation to the next: gold prospector, newspaper editor, Mississippi River steamboat pilot, lecturer, travel correspondent—and always, storyteller. It was while reporting on the California legislature in the early 1860s that he adopted the old river term "Mark Twain."

In 1870 Clemens married Olivia Langdon, a woman whose photograph he had fallen in love with long before he met her. Based in Hartford, Connecticut over the next two decades, Clemens led a joyous domestic life and a prolific literary one. Yet his happiness was not to last; bad investments left him bankrupt by the turn of the century, and the death of his beloved daughter, Susy, wounded him deeply. After several years in Europe, Clemens finally returned to America in 1900, his financial worries behind him. Soon thereafter, however, he would lose both his wife and another daughter, Jean. Samuel Clemens died at his Connecticut home, Stormfield, on April 21, 1910.

A man of no formal education, Twain's literary talent was recognized through honorary doctorates from Yale, Missouri, and Oxford Universities. His clarity of vision, his forthright honesty, his biting and yet humorous wit, have carved a place of honor for him in American literature.

Bibliographic Notes

When known, the date of writing—which differs from the publication date listed below—has been included in the text in parentheses after the citation. The date of writing of many of Twain's stories, which were collected posthumously, is unknown.

Twain's novels, stories, essays, letters, and speeches have been collected in at least fourteen different sets. Twain's designated biographer and editor was Albert Bigelow Paine, whose *Mark Twain: A Biography* appeared in 1912; Paine was followed by Charles Neider, editor of *The Autobiography of Mark Twain* (1959). Countless other biographical and critical works are available. Below is a partial list of Twain's works, many of which were published posthumously.

BOOKS
The Innocents Abroad, 1869
Roughing It, 1872
The Gilded Age, 1873
Sketches New and Old, 1875

The Adventures of Tom Sawyer, 1876
Stolen White Elephant, 1878
A Tramp Abroad, 1880
The Prince and the Pauper, 1882
Life on the Mississippi, 1883
The Adventures of Huckleberry Finn, 1884
A Connecticut Yankee in King Arthur's Court, 1889
The American Claimant, 1891
Tom Sawyer Abroad, 1894
Pudd'nhead Wilson, 1894
Personal Recollections of Joan of Arc, 1896
Tom Sawyer, Detective, and Other Stories, 1896
Following the Equator, 1897
The Man That Corrupted Hadleyburg and Other Stories and Essays, 1900
A Double Barrelled Detective Story, 1902
Adam's Diary, 1904
Eve's Diary, 1906
What Is Man?, 1906
Christian Science, 1907
A Horse's Tale, 1907
Captain Stormfield's Visit to Heaven, 1907
Is Shakespeare Dead?, 1909
Mark Twain's Speeches, 1910, 1923
The Mysterious Stranger and Other Stories, 1916
Mark Twain's Letters, 1917
Mark Twain in Eruption, 1922

Europe and Elsewhere, 1923
Mark Twain's Autobiography, 1924
More Maxims of Mark, 1927
Mark Twain's Notebook, 1935
Letters from the Earth, 1938
The Autobiography of Mark Twain, 1959
Mark Twain on the Damned Human Race, 1962
*A Pen Warmed Up in Hell: Mark Twain in
    Protest,* 1972
Mark Twain's Notebooks and Journals, 1975

PAMPHLETS
Concerning the Jews, 1899, 1934
To The Person Sitting in Darkness, 1901
To My Missionary Critics, 1901
A Dog's Tale, 1903
King Leopold's Soliloquy, 1905
The War Prayer (written 1905, but unpublished)

About the Editors

Stacey Freeman is an M.Phil. in Modern European History at New York University. She currently is writing a dissertation on infant mortality, eugenics, and the medicalization of German society during World War I and Weimar.

David Hodge is a television and theater director, a native Missourian, and lifelong devotee of Mark Twain.

THE CLASSIC WISDOM COLLECTION
OF
NEW WORLD LIBRARY

AS YOU THINK by James Allen. Edited and with an Introduction by Marc Allen. October, 1991.

NATIVE AMERICAN WISDOM. Compiled and with an Introduction by Kent Nerburn and Louise Mengelkoch. October, 1991.

THE ART OF TRUE HEALING by Israel Regardie. Edited and updated by Marc Allen. October, 1991.

LETTERS TO A YOUNG POET by Rainer Maria Rilke. Translated by Joan M. Burnham with an Introduction by Marc Allen. April, 1992.

THE GREEN THOREAU. Selected and with an Introduction by Carol Spenard LaRusso. April, 1992.

POLITICAL TALES & TRUTH OF MARK TWAIN. Edited and with an Introduction by David Hodge and Stacey Freeman. November, 1992.

THE WISDOM OF WOMEN. Selected and with an Introduction by Carol Spenard LaRusso. November, 1992.

New World Library is dedicated to publishing books and cassettes that help improve the quality of our lives.

For a catalog of our fine books and cassettes, contact:

New World Library
58 Paul Drive
San Rafael, CA 94903
Phone: (415) 472-2100
FAX: (415) 472-6131

Or call toll free:

(800) 227-3900
In Calif.: (800) 632-2122